Items should be returned on or before the last date shown below. Items not already requested by other borrowers may be renewed in person, in writing or by telephone. To renew, please quote the number on the barcode label. To renew on line a PIN is required. This can be requested at your local library.
Renew online @ **www.dublincitypubliclibraries.ie**
Fines charged for overdue items will include postage incurred in recovery. Damage to or loss of items will be charged to the borrower.

Leabharlanna Poiblí Chathair Bhaile Átha Cliath
Dublin City Public Libraries

Dublin City
Baile Átha Cliath

Central Library, Henry Street
An Lárleabharlann, Sráid Annraoi
Tel: 8734333

Date Due	Date Due	Date Due

D1345691

THE
LITTLE
BOOK
OF
COUNTY
DOWN

DOREEN MCBRIDE

The
History
Press

First published 2018

The History Press
The Mill, Brimscombe Port
Stroud, Gloucestershire, GL5 2QG
www.thehistorypress.co.uk

British Library Cataloguing in Publication Data.
A catalogue record for this book is available from the British Library.

ISBN 978 0 7509 8928 2

Typesetting and origination by The History Press
Printed and bound by TJ International Ltd

CONTENTS

ACKNOWLEDGEMENTS

I am grateful to my husband, George, for doing his best to knock what he considers nonsensical ideas out of my head; to my cousin, Vernon Finlay, for reading the manuscript and making helpful comment; and to my dear friend, Dr Joy Higginson, who responded to my husband's plea to 'give his head peace by acting as my minder while I did fieldwork'.

I am very grateful to the following people who provided information: the late Dr Bill Crawford; Dr William Roulston; the MCMS library at the Ulster American Folk Park, especially Christine Johnston; the Linen Hall Library, Newry Library and Banbridge Library; the Ulster Aviation Society; local historians Eric McIlroy, Ken and Florence Chambers, Plunkett Campbell, the late Ernest Scott, David Griffin, Jane Wright, Harry Allen, George Beattie, Michael and Norman Howland.

Thanks are also due to Arthur Chapman, past Principal of Friend's School; Linda Ballard UFTM; Dr Janine Paisley; the late Francey Shaw; the late David Elliott; Dr Tim Campbell; Eileen Finlay; Ali McCartney; Noel Killen for answering questions about Ballydugan Mill near Downpatrick; and Lady Anthea Forde could not have been more helpful regarding Seaforde Gardens and Butterflyhouse.

Further thanks go to Hector McDonnell, who gave me information, laughter and permission to reproduce his cartoon on page 53, and to Kirstyn Reilly for permission to use her cartoons on pages 19 and 32. All other illustrations are my own.

INTRODUCTION

The coat of arms below represents County Down, one of the six counties in the Province of Ulster that are part of the United Kingdom and Northern Ireland. The waves, ship and fish represent the county's rich maritime heritage, the sheaves the rich agricultural land, the flowers belong to the flax plant. County Down was once the centre of a thriving linen industry and linen threads are obtained from flax plants. The hand holding the crozier represents St Patrick, who started his missionary work near Strangford Lough. The stags represent peace and harmony between the Catholic and Protestant communities,

Coat of arms representing County Down.

while the Latin motto *Absque Labore Nihil* means 'Nothing Without Labour'.

There is one important fact missing from the coat of arms, namely the beauty of County Down. It's mainly rich farmland, formed by drumlins left over by the Ice Age. It contains two areas officially designated as Areas of Outstanding Natural Beauty, the Lagan Valley and Mourne Mountains.

County Down is bordered by County Antrim to the north, County Armagh to the west, County Louth to the south-west and the Irish Sea to the east.

County Down has excellent roads and connections with the rest of the world. It's sometimes quicker to travel from London to Belfast than from London to the north of England! In addition, it has good internal connections. It's possible to travel, by ferry, from Portaferry to Strangford, or from Greencastle to Greenore, in the Irish Republic. As a result of these connections and the resulting proximity of the law, inhabitants of County Down don't have the same opportunity to make and sell poteen (illegal 'home-made' alcohol) and smuggle animals and goods across a land border as those living in Fermanagh or Tyrone. The late Pat Cassidy, who lived in Lisnaskea, County Fermanagh, once said to me, 'In Down it's too risky to make an honest living making and selling poteen!' (That's illegal!)

There used to be a notable trade of smuggled goods by sea. The Brandy Pad through the Mourne Mountains was once used by smugglers to bring brandy, silk, tea, coffee and so on inland. Contraband was brought ashore and hidden in coastal caves before being dispersed.

County Down contains many interesting long-distance walks. There's a flat walk and cycle track along the Newry Canal. Part of the Ulster Way is beside a railway track that leads from Belfast to Bangor, making it possible to walk from say Holywood to Bangor and get a train back.

The River Lagan marks the boundary between Antrim and Down. Land to the south of the Lagan is in Down, that to the north is in Antrim. Strictly speaking, part of Belfast lies within the precincts of County Down, but it is such a large, interesting place that it was decided not to incorporate it in this book due to lack of space.

Two other glaring omissions, again due to lack of space, are the Ulster Folk and Transport Museum at Cultra and the Somme Museum on the road between Bangor and Newtownards. The Ulster Folk and Transport Museum is an open-air museum in two parts, one part dedicated to transport including a DeLorean and carriages from what is claimed to be the world's first long-distance electric tram; the other part recreates the landscape of 1900 with relocated farmhouses, and a village, Ballycultra, containing, among other exhibits, a silent picturehouse. It's a place to be savoured, not rushed, and it's well worth spending a day there.

The Somme Museum is also fascinating, giving, as it does, a glimpse of what it was like to live in a trench during the First World War. There's a lot of online information about both museums.

In addition, many towns have their own museums and tourist trails. It's always worth enquiring at local tourist information offices.

1

FASCINATING FACTS ABOUT COUNTY DOWN

Linen manufactured in County Down was used to cover the surface of Hurricane planes. Linen had the advantage of being strong and shells simply made a hole in it as they passed through. A strike wasn't as catastrophic as would have been the case if the plane had had metallic wings. These planes had to be placed under guard in the desert because camels liked licking their surface!

Noel Mitchel, who is in his 90s, remembers flying Spitfires towards the end of the war. He says, 'There was something about a Spitfire! It was easily handled, fast – a lovable plane!'

The last spitfires manufactured had a covering of thin aluminium but the tails and rudders continued to be covered in linen.

A 'Killinchy Muffler' is a hug during which the arms are placed around the neck. A 'Killinchy Waistcoat' is a closer hug during which the arms are placed around the waist. I wish I knew the origin of these old sayings and I'd be grateful to anyone who could enlighten me. Killinchy is a small village situated 2 miles from the southern side of Strangford Lough.

Come on ye girl ye, til I give ye a Killinchy waistcoat.

The St Patrick's Centre in Downpatrick is the only permanent exhibition centre in the world dedicated to the life of St Patrick. It's well worth a visit.

Several members of famous pop band Snow Patrol came from Bangor, County Down, and attended Bangor Grammar School.

Captain Moonlight, the notorious Australian bushranger, was born on Castle Hill, Rathfriland, in 1842. His real name was George Andrew Scott.

Charles de Gaulle has ancestors from County Down. They are buried in Lochinisland graveyard.

Dr Janine Paisley, who lives at Annacloy, near Crossgar, described the unfortunate effect of raising the water level of the river near Annacloy. Drinkers from Annacloy who required subsistence on Sundays, when Annacloy pubs were closed, used to run across the stepping stones in the river to drink and socialise in the Woodgrange. Raising the river's water level made the stepping stones impossible to use, so a quick dash across the river turned into a 5-mile journey by the road!

Catherine O'Hare was born in 1835 in Ballybrick, Annaclone, approximately 3 miles from Rathfriland. She was the mother of the first European baby born west of the Rocky Mountains. She travelled with her husband Augustus Schubert, and 200 other people who were prospecting for gold in a wagon train. They blazed the way for the Canadian Pacific Railway.

The first Norman windows in Ireland are in Inch Cistercian Abbey, which was founded in 1187 by John de Courcy, with monks from Furness Abbey in Lancashire. It is now a ruin in a beautiful setting on the banks of the River Quoile, near the place where it enters Strangford Lough.

Thomas Andrews, the Chief Naval Architect at Harland and Wolff (the company that built the *Titanic*), was born at Adara House, Comber, on 7 February 1873. He was one of four sons of a wealthy linen merchant and Lord Pirrie's nephew (the shipyard's chairman). He was seen as the natural successor to take control of Harland and Wolff when Lord Pirrie retired. He was a popular manager who cared for his workers and referred to them as 'my pals'.

Thomas married Helen Reilly Barbour in June 1908. She was the daughter of another wealthy Northern Irish linen family. The young couple moved to 12 Windsor Avenue, Belfast, but Thomas's heart lay in County Down. Every weekend was spent in Comber, where he sailed on Strangford Lough or played cricket. The couple had one daughter, Elba (Elizabeth Law Barbour Andrews).

Thomas was 39 when he was put in charge of the *Titanic*. It was the first ship for which he was responsible from start to finish. He sailed on *Titanic*'s ill-fated maiden voyage as head of the Harland and Wolff Guarantee Group (a specially selected group of workers who were on board to fix any snags – none survived). When the ship was sinking, Thomas showed concern for everyone except himself. He encouraged

See you, wee lad! I'm tellin' ye – the *Titanic* was all right when she left Belfast!

people to put on warm clothing and helped them into lifeboats. The officers say when last seen he was throwing deckchairs and other things to people in the water. His body was never recovered but a hall was built, by public subscription, in Comber, dedicated to his memory and opened in 1915. He is also remembered in his family's grave by a gravestone bearing the words, 'Pure, just, generous, affectionate and heroic. He gave his life that others might be saved.'

Professor Theodore Thomson Flynn came to Belfast from Tasmania in 1931 to take the chair of zoology at Queen's University Belfast, a post he held until his retirement in 1948. Professor Flynn was a respectable, well-regarded biologist and embryologist. His son, Errol Flynn, was a swashbuckling Hollywood idol and womaniser!

Errol helped his father finance a Tasmanian-styled house, called 'Kurrajong', at Kilclief, overlooking Strangford Lough. Until then Professor Flynn had lived in rented accommodation. 'Kurrajong' was the first house he owned. He lived there during most of the Second World War and after his retirement.

Professor Flynn's sober-looking house could not be more different from the one Errol shared with his hard-drinking, womanising friend, David Niven, in Malibu. They called it 'Cirrhosis-by-the-Sea'!

John Butler Yeats (1839–1922) was born at Tullylish. His father, William Butler Yeats, was rector of Tullylish Church of Ireland from 1834 until 1862.

John, a well-known artist, was the father of both the author William Butler Yeats (1865–1939) and the artist Jack Butler Yeats (1871–1957).

William Butler Yeats, poet and dramatist, was awarded the Nobel Prize for Literature in 1923. His brother Jack, who died in 1957, became a famous artist who received many honours, including the Legion of Honour and honorary degrees from universities such as Trinity College Dublin and the University of Ireland.

'The Man from God Knows Where' came from Bangor. His name was Thomas Russell. He was born in Cork and served in the British Army in India until he returned to Ireland and came to live in Bangor. He joined the United Irishmen, was involved in the 1798 Rebellion, and was captured, tried and hung outside Downpatrick Gaol (see Chapter 3).

The 1798 Rebellion was an uprising by Catholics and Presbyterians who didn't belong to the Established Church (the Anglican Church) and were thus denied education, couldn't hold a public office, and so on. Rents in Ireland were high and unfair taxes were placed on goods. The Uprising nearly succeeded and would have done if French reinforcements had been able to land. They were prevented because of a storm. More than 300,000 people died during that terrible time.

John Boyd Dunlop, who invented the pneumatic tyre for cars and bicycles, worked for several years as a vet in his brother James's veterinary practice in Downpatrick.

2

HISTORY

County Down was a famous seat of learning that contributed to Ireland's fame as a 'land of saints and scholars'.

Bangor's famous Monastery and School was founded by the missionary, Comgall, in AD 558. It became the parent of numerous educational and monastic establishments on the continent of Europe and in Scotland.

Bangor Abbey and schools prospered for nearly 200 years, with thousands of clerics and students resident at one time. Ireland suffered repeated raids from Norwegians and Danes during the early ninth century, which had a disastrous effect on the old abbey. The inspired leadership of Malachy O'Morgair during the early twelfth century resulted in a revival of its work. Its influence declined when the Irish Church became Anglo-Romanised and it was ended by King Henry VIII during the Dissolution of the Monasteries

John de Courcy, a prominent Anglo-Norman, caused far-reaching change in Ireland, including County Down. He defeated the Irish at Downpatrick in 1177 and gave his followers large estates. As a result, people with the surnames Savage, Martel, Ridal, Copeland, Jordan and Chamberlain, among others, settled in County Down. They built strong castles but couldn't resist persistent attacks by the Irish. Many adopted Irish manners and dress and conformed to Irish custom. The influence of the Anglo-Norman families had declined by the time Queen Elizabeth I came to the throne in 1558.

According to Irish custom, land didn't belong to the king – it belonged to the people. The Tanistry, that is the chieftainship of a tribe, didn't pass on by direct descent. Instead, it passed by election, but only relatives of the chief were eligible. That custom allowed the people to choose, as their leader, a chief who was strong. In 1589 the chieftainship passed to Con McBrien Fertagh O'Neill, the last chief of the Claneboye branch of the O'Neills. The chief didn't own the lands, he just held them as a trustee for his people. They disliked having to make fixed payments at fixed times, although they recognised they had a duty to support their lord. They willingly made irregular gifts, mostly in kind, and submitted to his often unreasonable demands.

The chiefs lived in stone castles while most people lived in huts made from branches stuck into the ground and bent inwards with wattle interwoven and built round with sods.

The O'Neills are an old family with roots going back into history. They have the reputation of being great warriors and politicians. The O'Neill of Clandeboye negotiated with Elizabeth I and she granted him lands, including the north and eastern parts of Down. He was bound to have felt annoyed because the land belonged to his ancestors in the first place! But needs must!

Laurence Eachard wrote in his book *Exact Description of Ireland* (1691):

> they are of middle stature, strong of body, of an hotter and moister nature than many other nations, of wonderful soft skins, and by reason on the tenderness of their Muscles, they excel in nimbleness and flexibility of all parts of the body; they are reckoned of a quick Wit, (although besotted to many follies) prodigal and careless of their lives, enduring Travel, Cold and Hunger: given to fleshly lusts, light of belief, kind and courteous to strangers, constant in Love, impatient of abuse, and injury, in enmity implacable, and in all affections most vehement and passionate. They are much delighted with Music, but especially the harp and Bagpipe; at the first many of them are very Skilful.

As for their Diet, they feed very much upon herbs especially watercresses; upon Mushrooms, Shamroots and Roots. They delight also in Butter tempered with Oatmeal; also in Milk, Whey, Beef-Broth, and Flesh ofttimes without any bread at all. As for their Corn, they lay it up for their horses, for whom they are very careful.

Queen Elizabeth I claimed possession of Ireland and waged a nine-year war (1593–1601) because she felt threatened. Her late sister's husband, King Philip of Spain, claimed her throne and Ireland helped him. When she won the war she did what kings and queens did in those days, she slaughtered as many natives as possible, confiscated their land and gave it to her soldiers.

She granted lands to the O'Neills but didn't see any reason not to grant them to somebody else as well. She had recognised the rights of Brian McFelim O'Neill, Chief of Southern Claneboye, to his territory and had given him a title, yet in 1571 she gave her secretary, Sir Thomas Smith, and his son the whole of Sir Brian's territory! Sir Brian was furious and protested but the queen refused to listen, so he laid waste to the territory and rendered it useless. A traveller described North Down as, 'Scarce and starving – a country without happiness and without religion.'

Sir Thomas Smith's son attempted to hold on to the land and was shot by a wild Irishman, and that was the end of that!

The Queen then granted part of the lands to her favourite, the Earl

The Irish'll help King Philip steal my throne. I'll have to knock the stuffing out of them!

of Essex. Sir Thomas Smith agreed to the arrangement and tried, for a short time, to hold on to the remainder of the territory. He failed, as did the Earl of Essex, so the territory in North Down fell back into Irish hands and the old tribal ways.

In 1586 Sir Con O'Neill played with his head, promised to be a submissive and loyal subject and formally surrendered his lands to the Queen. She gave them back to him under Letters Patent. He was succeeded by his nephew, Con O'Neill. Con's castle was a few miles from Belfast in the Castlereagh Hills, where Lagan College is situated today.

A few months before the death of Queen Elizabeth I, Con O'Neill had a drunken feast to celebrate Christmas in his castle. He ran out of wine – a tragedy at an Irish party – so he sent some of his servants into Belfast to buy more. They were drunk and met some soldiers who stole their wine as they were staggering home. A scuffle followed, during which one of the soldiers was wounded. He died during the night and the authorities interpreted the incident as 'levying war against the Queen'! Con O'Neill was promptly arrested and imprisoned in Carrickfergus Castle, which seems very unfair because he was at home during the scuffle.

By this time James I of England (who was also James VI of Scotland) was on the throne. Hugh Montgomery had powerful friends in the court of King James. He was an ambitious man, who wanted to own estates in Ireland. He made a bargain with Con O'Neill, promising to get him out of prison, and pardoned, in exchange for half his land! Con didn't like being incarcerated and was probably in fear of his life, so he readily agreed.

I'll get ye off the hook if ye give me half your land.
(Illustration by Kirstyn Reilly)

Hugh Montgomery hired Thomas Montgomery, who owned a vessel that traded with Carrickfergus, to spirit Con O'Neill away.

Thomas seduced the jailor's daughter. She 'borrowed' the key of the jail and smuggled it inside, hidden in the middle of a large cheese. Con O'Neill was released, spirited over to Scotland and taken to see King James, who pardoned him and gave his lands to Hugh Montgomery.

Hugh Montgomery honoured his agreement and re-conveyed half of his ancient lands back to Con O'Neill, but unfortunately Sir James Hamilton also had his beady eye on the rich land of County Down. He managed to convince King James that Hugh Montgomery had been given too much and the king transferred all the land into Sir James Hamilton's name, with the proviso that it was divided into three equal portions, one for Con O'Neill, one for Hugh Montgomery and one for Sir James.

Hugh Montgomery was raging, but wisely didn't protest because he still owned a large tract of land.

The sixteenth and seventeenth centuries marked the beginnings of Protestantism, when people were sickened by the corruption apparent in the Church. The Church split, giving rise to Protestantism. People who protested against the Church gave rise to the Reformation (the Roman Catholic Church reformed itself after the birth of Protestantism). In Scotland Protestants became known as Presbyterians because their Church was governed by a Presbytery.

England's King Henry VIII broke away from the Roman Catholic Church because of a disagreement with the Pope. He formed the Anglican Church, which became the established church when a Protestant monarch was on the throne.

In Scotland the Church's powerbase was threatened by Protestants because they would not recognise either the Pope or the Monarch as Head of the Church. They stated firmly, 'Jesus Christ is the only Head of the Church we will recognise.' Some even went as far as signing a covenant to that effect and became known as Covenanters. As a result, they were persecuted. It didn't matter who was on the throne, Roman Catholic or

Protestant monarch, Presbyterians, also known as Dissenters, were in big trouble, especially the hard-line Covenanters. It was against the law not to attend the established church. Dissenters could be severely fined, sent for trial, and, if found guilty, given a long prison sentence, transported, hung, hung drawn and quartered, or burnt at the stake. As a result, this period in Scotland's history is known as the Killing Times.

There had always been a close relationship between Scotland and the North of Ireland, so Hugh Montgomery and James Hamilton found it easy to encourage Scots to come to live in Ireland. It was easier to travel by boat across the sea than along rough paths through what was then the dense wooded land of either Scotland or Ireland. People living in Portpatrick regularly went to church in Donaghadee. Unfortunately, Ireland was in a bad state because it had been laid waste during the Elizabethan wars.

William Montgomery, a relation of Hugh Montgomery, wrote the Montgomery Manuscripts recording the family history between 1603 and 1706, and stated:

> In three parishes could not be found thirty cabins nor any stone walls but roofless churches and a few vaults at Grey Abbey, and a stump of an Old Castle in Newtown in each of which some gentlemen sheltered themselves at their first coming over.

Anglicans and Presbyterians weren't the only type of Protestantism. Huguenots were Protestants persecuted in France because of their religion. Approximately 10,000 settled in Ireland. They married locally, became members of the Anglican Church and were instrumental in the development of the linen industry, especially in Counties Antrim and Down.

County Down's thriving linen industry stimulated the development of an excellent transport system during the reign of Queen Victoria. It was cutting-edge, as shown by the Craigmore Viaduct outside Newry. It was designed for the Dublin and Belfast Junction Railway by Sir John MacNeill and constructed by William Dargan, a civil engineer known as the 'Father of Irish Railways'. Completed in 1852, the viaduct was recognised as one of the greatest engineering achievements of the age. It consists of eighteen gradually curved arches of 18.3m (60ft) span, crosses a long, deep valley and is 427m (1,400ft) long and 43m at its highest point. This was greater in dimension than anything attempted previously in Ireland. Today it carries trains travelling between Belfast and Dublin.

Quakers, like the Huguenots, settled in Ireland during the seventeenth century. They were influenced by the beliefs of George Fox, one of many people looking for a more satisfactory way to worship. He came from a very humble background in the north of England and found he could talk directly to Jesus through prayer. He thought, 'If I can talk to Jesus, so can everyone else. We don't need clergymen, music, fancy churches, any type of liturgy or sacraments. All we need is a bit of peace and quiet to have a private conversation with Jesus.' So, in 1652, he founded the Society of Friends in the north of England and it spread to Ireland during the Plantation of Ulster.

Arthur Chapman, a member of the Society of Friends, says, 'The Society of Friends was formed because many people were questioning authority. Religion became a major talking point in the way football is today!'

Members of the Society of Friends are called Quakers. They hold services in Meeting Houses and don't have music or clergymen. They sit quietly until the Spirit moves somebody to do something. They do, and have done, a lot of good work, including saving many lives during the Great Famine of 1845–1847.

The first Quaker settlement in Ireland was established in Lurgan, County Armagh, in 1654 by William Edmundson, who was born in 1627. He had served in Cromwell's Army. They spread quickly into County Down, with the main core of Quaker settlement in Ireland being along the Lower Bann and Lagan valleys.

There were two Quaker settlements near Banbridge, one at Moyallon, the other at Rathfriland. The one at Moyallon is still in good repair and used regularly by its small congregation. It's a beautiful building in a lovely setting with a peaceful churchyard, and is signposted on the road between Gilford and Lurgan.

Ireland's oldest surviving Quaker Meeting House is in Rathfriland; unfortunately, at the time of writing it is derelict.

Many of the Quakers who settled in Northern Ireland had, like William Edmundson, fought in Cromwell's army. Oliver Cromwell ran out of money to pay his army so he gave his soldiers small tracts of land in lieu of payment. As a result, the majority of Quaker settlers were smallholders. They must have been sickened by their experience of war because from that day to this they are pacifists. That doesn't mean they think they should be immune to the consequences of war. They don't run and avoid. They may refuse to fight, but they are willing to put themselves in danger by helping others as ambulance drivers, medics and so on. Today they are busy at work in Afghanistan, Syria and in other trouble spots throughout the world.

Quakers attempting to settle in Ireland found themselves in dangerous circumstances because the dispossessed Irish wanted their land back and the government found more reason to persecute them than the Ulster Scots. Both groups refused to recognise the king, dictator, Pope or anyone else as Head of the Church. Having that attitude was regarded as treason and punishable by transportation or death. In addition, Quakers refused to pay taxes to the established church and when they were sent for trial they got into more trouble because they refused to take oaths in court. To them oaths represented a double standard as they are honour-bound to tell the truth at all times, not just when standing holding a Bible in front of a jury. As a result, some Quakers looking for justice found themselves charged with contempt of court. As if that wasn't bad enough, they believe all men are equal, a terrible sin in those days! They wouldn't address anyone by using titles. They insisted on referring to everyone as thee or thou. Lords, ladies, clergymen, judges and anyone with any illusions of grandeur found that very offensive!

Quakers had a profound effect on the terrible conditions in prisons, which were dirty, overcrowded, full of rats and without proper sanitation or food. Elizabeth Fry, a Quaker, was responsible for reforming them. She visited Moyallon in 1827 and worshipped there in the Meeting House.

The Quaker graveyard at Moyallon reflects their belief in equality because all the gravestones are flat. Nobody has a headstone higher than anyone else, except those in a special section belonging to the Richardson family, and those who died in the armed forces.

Quakers believed that everyone should be literate and able to read the Bible. They placed emphasis on numeracy and observation of nature because numeracy leads to integrity in business and nature study is useful when farming. Many of the early Quakers were farmers.

Friends School in Lisburn is a surviving reflection of the recognition of the importance of education. It was founded in 1794 for Members of the Society of Friends, then, in the 1880s, they decided to admit other denominations.

3

PLACES

ARDGLASS

Ardglass gets its name from the Gaelic words 'Ard' and 'Glais', meaning the 'Green Height'. The name is apt because the town is built on a hill whose slopes surround a small but deep bay. It's in the Norman colony in Lecale, which was the strongest Norman colony in Ireland outside the Pale in Dublin. Ardglass harbour and that of Carrickfergus were the main ports of entry.

Today Ardglass is one of the leading fishing ports on the east coast of Ireland. There's evidence of human activity over 2,000 years as in 1851, while building Isabella's Tower on the highest point of the village, ancient funeral relics were found showing the mound on which it was built to be a prehistoric burial ground of an ancient chief, bard or warrior.

The village has eight archaeological sites in the area and two others nearby. There are a number of listed properties located on Castle Place, Kildare Street and The Crescent. St Nicholas Church, the King's Castle, Ardglass Castle, Isabella Tower, the derelict train station, the North Pier and the indoor docking station are also listed.

The inhabitants of Ardglass are rightly proud of the number of ancient monuments found within their village, which has arguably the most castles per square foot of any village in Ireland – six in all.

Personally, I've never seen so many structures looking like Elizabethan towers within such a confined area. Some appear to be in good condition while others are ruined. Two, that once stood side by side, The Newark and Horn Castle, were joined in the middle by Lord Charles Fitzgerald in 1790 and are now home to Ardglass Golf Club. The Newark was built around 1400, which makes the Golf Club's clubhouse the oldest in the world.

King's Castle overlooks the village and once consisted of two castles, King's Castle and Queen's Castle. In the 1820s Queen's Castle was undermined and fell into King's, reducing both to rubble. King's was later rebuilt in 1828.

There's an interesting circular walk around the village that can be obtained from the local Tourist Information office, or downloaded as an app on a smartphone.

BANBRIDGE

In 1690 there was a small settlement called Ballykeel around a ford across the River Bann, on the ancient Kings Road that ran from the south to the north of Ireland. It was here that King William III and his army crossed the River Bann in June 1690 on their way to the Battle of the Boyne. We know he crossed using the ford because archaeological excavation failed to reveal remnants of a bridge of the correct age. The ford was near the site of the present bridge, Dunbar Bridge, which is at the end of a track leading past Havelock Park on the Lurgan Road. It makes sense to think of an army crossing a river via a ford where the soldiers were able to spread out, as that would have been quicker than marching over a narrow bridge.

Ballykeel has been absorbed into Banbridge, a planter town, originally called Ballyvalley. It was founded by Moyses Hill (see Hillsborough). The Hill family were eventually awarded the title Marquess of Downshire, and the Downshires were responsible for laying out the town in its present form.

In the 1830s the design of stagecoaches changed; they became heavier and horses struggled to pull them up the steep hill in the middle of the town. Banbridge was in danger of being bypassed so his Lordship hired men to cut into the hill to make it more

Banbridge town in County Down.

accessible to stagecoaches. The two side streets were connected by a bridge over what residents refer to as 'The Cut', thought to be Europe's first flyover bridge.

A woman used to sell apples on the bridge and jingle her loose change in her pocket, so it became known as Jingler's Bridge. It's also known as the Downshire Bridge, after the Marquess who built it.

The Cut went through the old Brown Linen House, which was replaced by a brand-new building at the corner of Scarva Street. It was originally the Market House and later became the Town Hall. It has recently been renovated by Banbridge Council and now houses a Tourist Information Centre.

The Marquess also replaced the old wooden bridge at the foot of the town with a stone bridge, known locally as the Water Bridge. The town's name changed from Ballyvalley (also spelt BallyVally) to Banbridge in 1712, when the original wooden bridge was built.

The old coaching inn, The Bunch of Grapes, was a terrible place, filthy, full of lice, rats and generally falling down. His Lordship demolished it and built the Downshire Arms, a beautiful Georgian building at the top of the town.

Church Square contains a monument depicting polar bears known locally as the 'polar bears picnic'. It is dedicated to Francis Crozier (1796–1848), who discovered the Northwest Passage around the top of Canada. The monument is well worth a close look because it incorporates all sorts of things associated with Crozier's voyage, such as ropes and seals. Crozier was born in a large Georgian house opposite the monument, which is marked with a blue plaque.

Banbridge is a good shopping town with many pleasant places to eat. The Boulevard on the outskirts of the town contains a vibrant retail section, a multiscreen cinema and many eateries, including The Linen Hill, which received a very favourable mention in the *Sunday Times Good Food Guide*. The F.E. McWilliam Gallery (see Chapter 5) is nearby and well worth a visit.

BANGOR

Centuries ago Bangor, also known as 'Belfast by the Sea', was famous throughout Europe thanks to St Comgall, who founded his famous monastery there in the sixth century (see Chapter 2). It's situated on sandy Bangor and Ballyhome Bays and is the home of the Royal Ulster Yacht Club.

In a poll conducted by adult entertainment website Lovehoney, published in the *Belfast Telegraph* on 29 November 2013, Bangor was named the UK's sexiest town because its residents apparently spend the most on spicing up their sex lives. It's a popular place for retired couples to settle!

Today Bangor has two pleasant parks. Ward Park extends to 37 acres and is landscaped with ten tennis courts, a duck pond and a selection of birds housed in breeding pens. Pickie Fun Park has pedal boats shaped like swans, mini golf, playgrounds and a narrow-gauge railway.

CRAWFORDSBURN

There was an ancient highway between the Priory at Holywood (which gets its name from Holy Wood) and its parent Abbey at Bangor.

Crawfordsburn lies between Holywood and Bangor so it made a good stopping point before the advent of modern transport, which led to the establishment of a hostelry. The village of Crawfordsburn grew up around the Old Inn. It's a delightful place with whitewashed cottages and craft shops.

Nobody knows when the inn was established in Crawfordsburn, although it probably dates back to very early times, possibly to the establishment of nearby Christian institutions. What is known is that the Old Crawfordsburn Inn was founded in 1600, at the end of Queen Elizabeth I's reign. Records show the Old Crawfordsburn Inn was in its present form around in 1614. There is evidence of substantial additions made during the middle of the eighteenth century, which involved some of the upstairs bedrooms and the kitchen. The East Wing is modern, based on Irish Georgian style.

The Old Inn takes pride in owning a quern grindstone carved with the sign of the cross. It's in the corridor leading to the bar. It came from Bangor's ancient abbey and originally belonged to one of the students. The students had to grind their own meal supply as part of the discipline to which they were subjected. (Bangor Castle and Bangor Abbey have preserved many other treasures from the past.)

The Old Inn was used by smugglers right up to the end of the eighteenth century, with secret hiding places for contraband still being found well into the twentieth century!

The mail coach that connected with the sailing ship changed horses at the Old Inn. As a result, the Czar of Russia, Peter the Great, stayed there when he toured Ulster studying developments in the manufacture of damask linen, a textile for which the province is renowned. Many famous writers such as Anthony Trollope, Dean Swift, Charles Dickens, William Makepeace Thackeray and Alfred, Lord Tennyson have also been residents.

In 1958 C.S. Lewis and his wife Joy spent a belated honeymoon there, having what they described as 'a perfect fort-night'.

American visitors are particularly interested to hear that musician Paul Jones stayed at the Old Inn, as did the famous highwayman, Dick Turpin. He had to flee from England and spent his exile in Crawfordsburn. On a more serious note, part of King William III's army marched through the village on their way from Groomsport to join the main forces at Belfast.

DONAGHADEE

During the seventeenth and eighteenth centuries Donaghadee was one of the major ports between Ireland and the British mainland. Many of the Ulster/Scots planters came through Donaghadee port on their way to start a new life, which explains why many of the people living down the Ards Peninsula speak with a Scottish accent. Today the harbour with its lighthouse provides a pleasant walk.

The local pub, Grace Neill's, claims to have been founded in its present form in 1611. Local historian Harry Allen, however, says:

'I think that's a lot of nonsense! There's no doubt that it's a very old pub but when a past owner was asked to say when it first opened its door he pulled a year out of his head! It does date back to the 1600s and was originally called the King's Arms, a name it kept for more than 300 years. Grace Neill was given the pub by her father as a wedding present. She was a well-known fixture at the bar until she died in 1918, aged 98. Her ghost haunts the bar, where she is frequently seen dressed in Victorian garb, tidying up and washing glasses or sitting smoking her clay pipe.'

DOWNPATRICK

Downpatrick is closely associated with St Patrick (see Chapter 4). The town is compact, with the sites of interest within easy walking distance. There's a high cross, dating back to AD 900, standing in front of the cathedral. It's been moved several times, having formerly served as the market cross in front of the Assembly Rooms. It was put in its present situation in 1897 and Down Arts Centre is now housed in the old Assembly Rooms.

Two hoards of gold bracelets were found in Down Cathedral's churchyard during the 1950s. They're kept in Down Museum, which is on the street behind the cathedral in the old County Down Gaol.

The gaol opened in 1796 and closed in 1830. It housed many thousands of prisoners, including those sentenced to be transported to New South Wales. When the building stopped functioning as a gaol it housed the South Down Militia as well as troops during the First and Second World Wars. Today it contains over 10,000 objects and 40,000 photographs.

Northern Ireland's only working heritage railway is in Downpatrick. It travels between Downpatrick, Magnus Barefoot's Grave (Magnus Barefoot was a Viking king, who was killed on the site of his gave in AD 1001 while stealing cattle to feed the crews of his ships) and Inch Abbey (see Chapter 1).

There's an area known as The Grove where John Wesley (1703–1791), the founder of Methodism, preached on several occasions. The trees were planted by Edward Southwell in 1740.

Denver's Coaching Inn is an interesting building, full of old-world charm with a worn stone tablet in the gable wall inscribed 'John and Ann McGreevy 1642'. A sixteenth-century fireplace has survived to the present day, although it has been altered.

DROMORE

Dromore's name comes from the Irish *Droim Mór*, meaning large ridge. It's a small town with an interesting history.

The cathedral's site is thought to date back to St Patrick. It has an ancient, mutilated Celtic cross in its churchyard. The cross was originally sited in the square. It became derelict, was eventually re-sited and renovated by what was then Banbridge

District Council. They inserted a memorial to their good work in the middle of it. Unfortunately, the cross's base couldn't be recovered because it had been built into the stairway of the town hall!

Dromore has a fine example of a motte and bailey, built during the thirteenth century by John de Courcy, a fine example of Anglo-Norman fortification. It is on high ground within a semi-circular loop in the River Lagan. The bailey, or lower courtyard, was protected by a palisade. The mound gave good vision and a reasonable field of fire, and is thought to have been used as an archery tower. The Pipe Rolls in Queen's University Belfast show the troops kept live animals for food within the palisade. There's a lovely view over the town and upper Lagan Valley from the top of the mound.

Dromore has the remains of an Elizabethan tower house, which was once part of a castle. When it became derelict a local businessman, by the name of Harrison, was building new business premises and thought he'd recycle the castle's stones. He'd removed the portcullis and entrance before the Bishop found out and arrived to stop him!

There are old stocks outside the old town hall, now the library, in what was the market square. The local high school sometimes used them to raise money by 'locking' members of staff in them and charging pupils to throw wet sponges at them.

GREYABBEY

Greyabbey is on the eastern side of Strangford Lough. It contains one of Ireland's most complete Cistercian Abbeys, founded in 1193 by John de Courcy's wife,

Greyabbey's dead-on. (Illustration by Kirstyn Reilly)

Affreca, along with monks from Holm Cultran, in Cumberland. The abbey was dissolved in 1537 during King Henry VIII's Dissolution of the Monasteries and as if that wasn't bad enough, the O'Neills burnt the building to keep it from being used by English colonists during the reign of Queen Elizabeth I (see Chapter 2). The gable of the refectory is complete and contains three beautiful lancet windows.

Greyabbey has several nice places to have a meal and a number of antique shops. They are not always open so it's as well to check.

HILLSBOROUGH

Hillsborough owes its origin to Queen Elizabeth I. She gave vast tracts of land in Ireland to Moyses Hill, an officer with the Earl of Essex. Sent by the Queen to suppress the rebellious Irish, he arrived in 1573 and acquired 40,000 acres in County Down, including, in 1611, the Hillsborough area. His son, Peter Hill, built a fort, the church (in 1636) and made plans for the village. (There's a lane leading to the fort and the church across the road from the palace.)

Wills Hill, Lord Hillsborough (1718–1793) inherited the estates in 1742. He held many appointments, the most important being that of Secretary of State for the American colonists. As a result, Benjamin Franklin stayed with him in Hillsborough for five days in 1771. The two men, however, grew to hate each other. Franklin said Hill regarded him as 'an orange that would yield no more juice and therefore not worth more squeezing'. It's been suggested the dislike Hill and Franklin had for each other was a contributory factor in the American War of Independence. In spite of that failure, Wills Hill was granted the title Marquess of Downshire in 1798.

Hillsborough's an attractive Plantation village. It looks like an English village with well-preserved Georgian houses, an ancient market place (the Shambles) a beautiful Anglican parish church and a castle, the Marquess of Downshire's home.

When the Hills left Northern Ireland, the castle became the resident of the Governor of Northern Ireland. Now it's the residence of the Secretary of State and other visiting dignitaries. The royal family stay there when they are in the Province and it has recently been given the status of a Royal Palace. It is open to the public, but it's as well to check because it may be booked out, or there could be a royal in residence.

Hillsborough Castle is surrounded by a beautiful garden, complete with swans and trees planted by visiting royalty. Prince Charles had an input into the planting and of the terrace at the back of the building.

Queen Elizabeth, the Queen Mother's sister, was the wife of the first Governor of Northern Ireland, the 3rd Duke of Abercorn. As a result, our present Queen and her sister Princess Margaret spent a lot of time in Hillsborough Castle and they loved it.

The Georgian terrace houses on the left side of Main Street (when travelling downhill) have large gardens that back onto the castle grounds. My friend, Dawn Mitchell, and her husband live in one of these houses. The end of their garden is bounded by a high stone wall that forms the boundary of Hillsborough Castle. (Dawn's garden is open to the public under the RHS Open Garden scheme and at other times by appointment.)

The boundary wall provides difficulties for young swans flying towards the lake in the castle grounds. They are tired, see the lake and land on Dawn's lawn. She believes they think they can have a rest then walk to the lake. Unfortunately, they can't get up enough momentum to clear the wall and are stuck.

The first time that happened Dawn contacted the USPCA and a helpful man came out. He looked at the swan, marched purposely towards it, threw a rug over its head, bundled it up, put it in the back of his van, took it to Hillsborough Forrest and released it on Hillsborough Lake.

Now if a swan lands in her garden Dawn doesn't wait for the USCPA! She gets a rug, throws it over the swan's head, puts it into her car and takes it to Hillsborough Lake. I should stress that Dawn has a great gift with animals and I don't advise going near swans. They may attack humans and their wings are strong enough to break legs!

Hillsborough Lake is very pleasant. It has a crannog (see Loughbrickland) and is encompassed by a path.

The Downshires were good landlords, who married for money with one exception. One of the younger sons of the 4th Marquis of Downshire, Lord Arthur William Hill (1846–1931), married for love! His first marriage, in 1873, to Annie Nisida Denham Cookes, daughter of Lieutenant-Colonel George Denham Cookes, was a marriage of convenience. She died a year later, shortly after the birth of their only son.

Lord Athur Hill fell in love with his sisters' friend, Annie Fortesque Harrison. She was a beautiful and talented musician, but she wasn't in the same social league as Lord Arthur. In spite of the differences in their circumstances, the young couple had a lot in common and fell deeply in love.

It is said that one evening Annie overheard somebody saying, 'Anyone can see Lord Hill is greatly attracted to Annie. She obviously reciprocates his feelings. She should catch herself on. She's not a suitable candidate to be the wife of a lord. If she really cared for him she'd go away and leave him free to find a suitable wife.'

Annie was very upset but felt the gossips were right, so she disappeared without leaving a forwarding address.

Lord Hill was heartbroken. He did his best to find her, but she must have told her friends she didn't want to see him and he failed miserably.

Two years later one of Annie's compositions, 'In the Gloaming', was published. It became a hit tune and Sir Arthur was able to trace her through her publishers. He flew to her side and insisted she come back to Hillsborough and marry him.

In the Gloaming

In the gloaming, oh my darling, when the lights are dim
and low,
And the quiet shadows flicker, softly come and softly go,
When the winds are sobbing faintly, with a gentle
unknown woe,
Will you think of me and love me, as you did once long ago.

In the gloaming, oh my darling, think not bitterly of me,
'Tho I passed away in silence left you lonely set you free,
For my heart was filled with longing, what had been
could never be,
It was best to leave you thus dear, best for you and best for me.

It's said that Annie and Sir Arthur's ghosts haunt Hillsborough.
You may hear the sound of hooves on the street leading to the
castle and see a coach and four coming up the hill. It stops and
a young man helps a beautiful young lady to alight. They look
so happy it would make your glass eye water!

Nigel McKelvey has an apartment in an old Georgian building
adjacent to the castle. He once heard the sound of a coach and
horses passing by, but when he looked out of the window there
was nothing there.

Annie's organ, which was given to her as a present by Lord
Arthur, is now in Hillsborough Parish Church.

HOLYWOOD

In ancient times Holywood was called Ballyderry, meaning
'townland of the oak wood'.

St Laiseran founded a church there during the seventh
century. A friary was founded on the site of the old church in
1200, when the name changed to the Latin, *Sanctus Boscus*,
or Holy Wood. This establishment, like the one in Bangor,
suffered from raids by Norsemen and the struggles between
the O'Neills and the English.

During the mid-nineteenth century, the railway was built along the North Down coastline and Holywood became the place where Belfast's industrial elite wanted to live. As a result, they built magnificent mansions in the surrounding area and parts of the town have today been designated as a conservation area. The road between Belfast and Bangor is the site of so many mansions it is known as Northern Ireland's Gold Coast.

Holywood is proud of its maypole; it's the oldest surviving one in Ireland and is still used every May Day!

I danced round the maypole when I was a child. Each dancer was given a ribbon to hold while a man called out directions. As we danced round in time to the music we wrapped our ribbons in a pattern around the maypole. At first we got it all wrong! There was a great deal of laughter and we were told how to put things to rights. Eventually we succeeded and the maypole became wrapped up in ribbon and we became closer and closer to it as the ribbon got shorter. There was a lot of laughter when we were clustered close together and were told to turn in the opposite direction to the one in which we had been facing and by following directions we unwrapped the maypole. After that other children were given a turn.

KILKEEL

Kilkeel gets its name from the twelfth-century church, St Colman's, *cill-caol*, which means 'church of the narrow place'. The ruins of a church dedicated to St Colman Del Mourne, built in 1388, are on a narrow site above the town.

Kilkeel is the centre of the Kingdom of Mourne with a harbour containing one of the largest fishing fleets in Ireland, where it's often possible to buy fresh fish.

An elderly woman, known as the 'Knicker Lady', used to stand beside the harbour at weekends. She sold very strong working boots and was called the 'Knicker Lady' because she used to flash them when she hitched up her ample skirts and gave people change out of an elasticated leg of her knickers!

I remember the 'Knicker Lady'.

The graveyard of the oldest church in Kilkeel contains the mass grave of seven unidentified bodies of people who were drowned at sea on 3 November 1916. It was a wild night, with the worst storm seen for seventy years, with howling winds causing gigantic waves to break around the County Down coast. The SS *Retriever*, a coal boat, got into difficulties and attempted to find safety in Newry, which is at the head of Carlingford Lough.

The shipping lane out of the lough is very narrow. It was 8 p.m. when the SS *Connemara*, belonging to the London and North Western Railway, was in the shipping lane on its normal route to Holyhead. The *Retriever* hit the *Connemara* amidships and cut her in two. All ninety-four passengers aboard her were drowned.

The *Retriever* was badly damaged; water rushed into its engines, causing them to explode. The crew perished, with only one survivor, James Boyle, who was 21 years of age.

At the time of the collision James was in the bottom of the *Retriever* shovelling coal, when he heard a loud bang and people screaming. Water started coming in. He rushed to the top deck to see what was going on. He slipped and fell into a lifeboat, which crashed into the sea and was smashed to smithereens. He grabbed a plank and held on for grim death until he eventually washed up on the shore between Greencastle and Kilkeel. He was too exhausted to move or even cry for help. Eventually William Hanna saw a bundle of clothes lying on the shore, investigated, found James and took him to hospital. He escaped with a few minor injuries.

Many people said they'd had warnings of the disaster. James Boyle himself claimed to have seen the Ghost Ship, the *Lord Blaney* (see Chapter 9), while Mrs A. Small, of Cleveland Street, said she'd had a vivid dream during which she saw herself on the Greenore steamer, heard an explosion and found herself in the sea along with her daughter and dead bodies. She told her friends and relatives she would not travel on the Greenore steamer 'for love or money'. They laughed at her, but in retrospect she was right!

Mary Angela McCardle, from Mulladuff, County Monaghan, was travelling to join her relatives, who lived in Chicago. Her sister-in-law had a nightmare in which she saw Angela drown, and Angela was one of the victims.

The following story was recorded in 1968 in Donaghmoyne Parish Magazine. Simon McGarrell was on holiday and staying with his mother. The night before he was due to travel back to mainland on the Connemara, his friends held a party. They were cycling home when they saw a White Lady pass through the wheels of his bicycle and disappear into a pile of stones. They warned Simon, who laughed, set sail next the evening on the *Connemara* and was drowned.

Bodies and wreckage washed up along the shore for days after the disaster. Fifty-eight came ashore quickly, others took weeks to arrive. Many bodies were unrecognisable because they'd been charred by the explosion.

A temporary morgue was set up in Nicolson's potato shed near Kilkeel. (It still exists – it's a long, narrow building sited on the left-hand side of the main road when travelling from Greencastle to Kilkeel. The doors are at the front of the building on the side nearest the road.) An inquest was held in Kilkeel on 6 November 1916. The coroner and members of the jury visited the scene of the tragedy to see the bodies and wreckage that had been collected.

The verdict was 'deathly drowning' caused by collision of the ships. It was the worst tragedy to hit the County Down coast.

People came from all over Ireland to identify their loved ones. Annie Duffy's mother came from Sligo to recover her daughter's body. She lifted the girl's skirts and found the gold souvenirs that had been sewed into the hem of her petticoats.

The London and North Western Railway Company paid for the transport of Annie's body back home. Her coffin was taken from the morgue by horse and cart to Greencastle, by ferry across to Greenore, and by guard's van to Sligo, while her mother travelled first class from Greenore to Sligo by train.

The Kilmorey Arms Hotel in Kilkeel is interesting. It was an old coaching inn built in 1843 at a cost of nearly £2,000. The *Picturesque Handbook of Carlingford Lough*, dated 1846, states:

The Kilmorey Arms Hotel has all the attributes of an English Country Inn and what higher praise can be bestowed upon it? It is snug and home-like possessing a combination of comfort and elegance, and yet complete in all its appointments, being moreover totally divested of the bustle and numerous inconveniences of an ordinary hostelry. Its charges too are very moderate ... we strongly recommend it accordingly for its fare.

The same comments are true today. It is a delightful family-run hotel with comfortable accommodation and helpful staff, who, if you want to climb the Mournes, will arrange transport there and back. It has had many distinguished guests, including Sir Winston Churchill and President Eisenhower.

LOUGHBRICKLAND

Loughbrickland can trace its origins back to Bricu, one of the Men of Ulster featured in the Ulster Cycle of Tales recorded by monks during the eighth century.

By all accounts Bricu was a nasty piece of work, guaranteed to cause trouble. He aimed to get father fighting son, mother fighting daughter, the Men of Ulster fighting each other and the women so angry that their breasts banged together with rage! He met his just deserts as he watched the final battle of the Tain, a war over who should own the Brown Bull of Cooley. He loved a good fight and laughed his head off as he watched warriors being slaughtered. Unfortunately, he laughed too loudly for too long as the Brown Bull went berserk and killed him!

The Ulster Cycle of Tales says Bricu lived on a crannog in the middle of Loughbrickland. (He also owned land at Dundrum, the scene of Bricu's Feast, but that's another story.)

A crannog is an artificial island formed from rocks, stones, mud and anything else in the middle of a lake. It was a good defensive position because enemies couldn't approach without being seen. Boats or 'causeways' were used to get to it. The 'causeway' was along a mat, woven from reeds and secured at either end by structures in exactly the same way that tent pegs are used today. If you were being pursued by an enemy you could run across the 'causeway' and remove the pegs so your enemy fell into the water!

The village of Loughbrickland is named after Loughbrickland. Its history is similar to that of many other villages and towns in County Down in that it dates from the Plantation. It was founded by Sir Marmaduke Whitechurch in the late 1580s when

They called Loughbrickland after me! It must have been because of my good looks.

he received land around the area and was ordered to organise the production of clothes for the army.

Sir Marmaduke was a Protestant but, in 1704, his great-granddaughter, Mary, married a Catholic, Sir John Whyte of Leixlip Castle. His father, Charles, had fought with King James against King William of Orange at the Battle of the Boyne, so his lands had been confiscated. His son, Sir John, was a clever politician who managed to negotiate the family lands back after his father died in 1697 despite two great disadvantages, namely he'd fought on the wrong side during the Williamite Wars, and he was a Catholic!

Another unusual fact about the Loughbrickland property is that it passed down through the female line. As a result, Whyte rather than Whitechurch became the name associated with the area.

Captain Nicholas Charles Whyte was an able politician who contributed to getting the Catholic Emancipation Act through Parliament in 1829. After that date everyone was allowed to be educated and it was possible to build all types of churches and attend worship openly.

Incidentally, Captain Nicholas was the first Catholic to become High Sheriff of Down (in 1830). That was another tremendous achievement and the Whyte family were the only landlords in the district to reduce rents during the Great Famine.

Captain Nicholas began thinking about building a Catholic Church in Loughbrickland in 1824 when he wrote to the Marquess of Downshire asking for a donation towards the costs. The Marquess of Downshire readily agreed.

Captain Nicholas died in 1844 and the estate passed to his 18-year-old son, John Joseph. John Joseph continued his father's work on Catholic emancipation by donating land on which a Catholic Church was built and by giving land to the priest to be used as a garden.

Loughbrickland has not been destroyed by modernisation. Georgian buildings, complete with beautiful fanlights, are still intact and several old water pumps and horse's drinking troughs are lovingly preserved in gardens.

The Whyte family still live in the 'Big House'; they remain a hard-working and generous family, who have developed their Court Yard into 5-star self-catering accommodation and, with help from Banbridge Council, turned what was originally known as 'The Ride' into a pleasant trail now called 'The Walk'. It follows the estate boundary and is open to the public.

NEWCASTLE

Newcastle gets its name from the New Castle built by the Magennises, the Lords of Iveagh, in 1588 at the point where the Shimna River runs into the sea. Today it is one of the most popular seaside and golfing resorts in Northern Ireland. It's in a beautiful situation nestled at the foot of the Mountains of Mourne with a 3-mile beach stretching towards Dundrum.

NEWRY

Tradition says that St Patrick planted a yew tree at the head of Carlingford Lough that pointed its dark leaves towards the heavens for over 700 years and gave the city its name.

Newry's Cathedral is a stunning granite building dedicated to St Patrick and St Colman. It was the first Catholic Cathedral opened after the Act of Catholic Emancipation in 1829.

Newry is known as the Frontier Town because it was near the English Pale and today it is near the border between Northern Ireland and the Irish Free State.

Dean Swift visited the town and doesn't appear to have liked it because he wrote:

High Church, low steeple,
Dirty streets and proud people.

Today the people are rightly proud of Newry, which has acquired city status.

Newry has a vibrant arts scene including excellent theatrical productions in the Sean Hollywood Arts Centre and the historic Town Hall, where it's possible to enjoy top-class musicals, dramas and comedy.

Bagenal's Elizabethan castle (see Chapter 10) was rediscovered in 1996 entombed inside the nineteenth-century Victoria bakery, which, incidentally, was still baking corn bread. Also known as 'yellow bread', it was introduced in Ireland during the Great Famine, and produced continuously into the 1990s.

The castle was a fortified house built on the site of an old Cistercian Abbey. The original plans have survived and restoration work uncovered some of the old castle's original features, including fireplaces and an oven. The building has been restored and now houses an interesting museum.

NEWTOWNARDS

Newtownards, at the head of Strangford Lough, is one of James I planter towns (see Chapter 2). In earlier times it was a small village clustered around a Dominican Friary, dedicated to St Columba, and said to have been founded by the Earl of Ulster, Walter de Burgo.

Newtownards is dominated by Scrabo Tower in a prominent position on the hill above the town, so it dominates the skyline for miles around. It resembles an Elizabethan tower house, but is comparatively modern as it was erected in 1851 and dedicated to the memory of the 3rd Marquess of Londonderry.

Folklore states that the granite outcrop on which Scrabo Tower stands was once the home of Sean Macananty, the King of the Northern Fairies. A cairn marked the spot until 1855, when it disappeared, and stories are the only thing left of Sean's existence.

Folklore states that when you see Scrabo Hill you should greet Sean or he could take offence and bring you bad luck! All that's necessary is to say something along the lines of 'Good morning Sean' or 'How are you Sean?' or in local parlance, 'How's about ye Sean?'

PORTAFERRY

Portaferry is situated at the southern end of the Ards Peninsula.

A narrow channel forms the entrance to Strangford Lough. It's 5 miles long and half a mile wide, and separates Portaferry from Strangford. The two villages are connected by a car ferry. The rush of the tide up the narrow channel means the ferry can't sail straight across the lough but is pulled by the flow in a wide semicircle either up or down the lough depending on the water flow.

Portaferry has an interesting aquarium, Exploris Aquarium and Seal Sanctuary, where the family can learn more about marine life in the lough and the Irish Sea. It has, among other exhibits, a large open tank where it's possible to come up close and personal with skates (they like having their heads stroked!).

There's a Marine Biology Station, belonging to Queen's University Belfast in Portaferry near the ferry terminal. As a result, visitors to the village are sometimes surprised to see students wearing wellingtons and carrying buckets wandering along the shore. They aren't mad – they're simply doing fieldwork studying the rich fauna associated with the shore.

A walk up Windmill Hill provides beautiful views.

ROSTREVOR

Rostrevor is an attractive resort, approximately 2 miles from Warrenpoint on the South Down coast.

The oral tradition states that during the Elizabethan age a beautiful lady called Rose married her lover, a man by the name of Trevor. The young

Rose Trevor must have been a real humdinger.

couple made their home in County Down. They became famous among Elizabethan gentry because of their hospitality and the beauty of their home's location. The village that grew around their home was referred to as Rose Trevor and through time the name changed to 'Rostrevor'.

The coastline between Rostrevor and Warrenpoint is lined with luxury houses. There is only one word possible for the location and that is 'spectacular'.

A path through beautifully wooded grounds leads up Slievemartin to a huge great boulder known as the Cloughmore.

Finn MacCool and the Cloughmore Stone
Folklore says Finn, the Irishman giant, stood on Slieve Foy, on the other side of Carlingford Lough, and threw the boulder at Benandonner, the Scottish giant. He missed and the Cloughmore Stone landed on the top of Slievemartin. That didn't matter because Benandonner was so frightened by the sight of the huge boulder flying through the air that he fled back to Scotland!

The Location of Narnia
Another beautiful walk goes along the Kilbroney River and through the Fairy Glen, which is said to be the location of Narnia in *The Lion, the Witch and the Wardrobe* by C.S. Lewis.

The Vampire Tree
Folklore says an African doctor called Mogh-Dhu and his followers came to live in the neighbourhood. They worshipped demons and were defeated by Christian missionaries in a battle of good against evil. Mogh-Dhu attempted to escape by climbing into a small opening in a tree. He died there because he couldn't get out. His tissues were absorbed by the tree, which became evil. Birds stayed away from it and people learned not to go close because the lower branches curled round them, and Mogh-Dhu's vampire sucked their blood out before throwing their lifeless bodies onto the ground beneath. Thankfully, the ancient Vampire Tree blew down in the Big Wind on 6 January 1839. Its growth rings showed it to be hundreds of years old.

St Bronagh's Bell

Another local tale tells of Fergus, the young chieftain of Glen Secis, who flew into a temper when his favourite hound was accidentally killed by Chief Artan of Lecale. Fergus killed Artan's hound then placed an arrow in his bow, fired it at Artan and hit him in the chest. Fergus picked up his dead dog, put it over his shoulder, left Artan for dead and, filled with grief, ran down the mountainside.

At first Fergus was glad he'd avenged the death of his dog, then he was sorry and became guilt-ridden. As a penance he presented a bell and twelve candlesticks to St Bronagh and her religious community.

St Bronagh had a chamber formed between two branches of a young oak tree near the church, and hung the bell there. The sound of the bell drifting over the glen comforted Fergus who, as a further act of atonement, resigned as leader of his clan, donned a hair shirt, sandals and a sackcloth coat and began travelling as a pilgrim.

Fergus travelled through many lands until he was an old bent man nearing the end of his life. He returned home and was horrified to find the place had been ravaged by Danes. The church and convent were in ruins and all his friends were either dead or had fled. As he hobbled through the ruined settlement he saw the ancient cross with a white-haired old man kneeling at its foot. It was Artan, who explained his people had found him alive, although badly wounded, and had nursed him back to health. Fergus was overjoyed to hear he didn't have blood on his hands and Artan had forgiven him. He died a short time afterwards in Artan's arms.

The bell continued to ring and over time people forgot where it was and began to think of its chimes as a warning because they could only be heard during storms. Many unsuccessful attempts were made to find the bell. They failed because the sound echoed around the glen. Eventually the sound stopped and the glen's people worried because they no longer received warnings. Nobody knew why the bell stopped ringing and eventually people living in the glen forgot about it, or, if they did hear the old tale they dismissed it as a foolish folktale.

There was dreadful storm in 1885 and a large oak tree near the old church in Kilbroney cemetery blew down. When workmen were cutting it up they sawed off two large branches near the top of the tree and found a recess in the trunk with the bell inside. The bell didn't have a tongue because the ring holding it had been worn away and it had fallen down to the bottom of the recess.

The bell was examined by antiquarians, who said it was one of the earliest Christian consecrated bells found in Ireland. It had tolled over the glen for more than 1,000 years before falling silent. It's been renovated and is now in the Catholic church at Rosetrevor.

The Ross Monument

The Ross Monument is about a quarter of a mile west of the centre of Rostrevor. General Ross, a native of the village, distinguished himself during the American War of Independence. He was responsible for burning down the White House!

STRANGFORD, STRANGFORD LOUGH AND CASTLE ESPIE

Strangford is a small village on the shores of Strangford Lough, opposite Portaferry and connected with it by a car ferry. It takes 8 minutes to cross from one side of the lough to the other. Going by road would take 90 minutes (it's 47 miles). Strangford's a pleasant village with Georgian houses and a beautiful situation.

The Cuan, a family-run hotel in Strangford, has one of the doors featured in *Game of Thrones*.

Strangford Lough is fascinating. The narrow opening to the lough causes a great tidal rush through its narrow entrance, which was used for the aborted SeaGen installation project. SeaGen was a tidal turbine that generated power by using rotors mounted in water. The trouble was that a large installation of this type interfered with the marine life of the lough and it was felt that smaller turbines utilising the lough's smaller tidal eddies would be less destructive and more efficient.

Strangford Lough is very interesting because it's situated where currents coming up from the equator meet those coming down from the Arctic. As a result, all kinds of unexpected flora and fauna may be found. The inland end of the lough is a bird sanctuary, which is of great importance to wintering waterfowl. It is one of the most important areas for birds in Ireland, at peak times hosting more than 20,000 waterfowl and over 40,000 waders.

Castle Espie (the name means the Bishop's Castle, although the castle no longer exists) is 3 miles from Comber and is a wetland reserve managed by the Wildfowl and Wetlands Trust. It was opened as a Wildfowl and Wetlands Trust Centre on 4 May 1990 by Lady Scott. The site had previously served as part of a farm and a limestone quarry with lime kilns for producing lime from limestone, a brick works and a pottery.

Castle Espie has the largest collection of ducks, geese and swans in Ireland. It provides a great family day out with free parking, hides, woodland walks, exhibition areas, events, activities, the Graffan Gallery, a shop and café, as well as the reserve containing ducks and other birds. It's an early wintering site for almost the entire Arctic population of pale-bellied brent geese.

Castle Espie is just shy of 3 miles from Comber along the Ballydrain Road on the shores of Strangford Lough, travelling towards Strangford.

Daft Eddy

A causeway leading to Daft Eddy's (also spelt Eddie) pub and restaurant is further along the road leading to Castle Espie. It's near the village of Whiterock.

Daft Eddy had an interesting history. He was a real person but the place and origin of his birth is a mystery. All that is known is that one day a boat appeared when Robert Barbour was out fishing; a baby was thrust into his arms and the boat disappeared as quickly as it had come. Robert took the baby home to his wife, and when they unwrapped the blankets they found a note asking them to call the baby Eddy, to take good care of him and to use the £50 found enclosed as a contribution towards his keep, and that they would receive more money each year for the baby's upkeep.

Robert and his wife were delighted. They had longed for a child of their own but had been unable to have one. As for the money – they had never seen so much in all their lives!

Eddy was a strange child. He never worked, he just passed his time wandering around the lough learning about birds and flowers. The locals said he was simple so he became known as 'Daft Eddy'. His adopted mother doted on him and he was spoilt rotten.

Eddy grew up to be an affectionate young man and because he was simple he became involved with the smugglers of Strangford Lough, who were called the 'Merry Hearts of Down'. They were far from 'merry' because they were ruthless, hard men. They tortured and killed people who betrayed their activities and used caves around Down's coast to hide contraband. They terrorised the local population when they extended their activities and became involved in robbery and violence as well as smuggling.

Thomas McFadden was a rich man, a magistrate with a beautiful daughter, called Martha. Eddy fell in love with her. She never knew because he was too shy to say anything, but she was a nice girl who treated him kindly on the few occasions she saw him. Eddy was horrified when he discovered the 'Merry Hearts of Down' intended to attack her home. He warned her father, who

Poor Daft Eddy – the smugglers done him in!

prepared for the attack and repulsed it. Guessing that Eddy had told the magistrate, the smugglers caught and tortured him, leaving him for dead. He was carried home to Island Magee, where he died surrounded by his many friends. His last words were, 'Mother, I'm goin' to Martha. Place me in my boat. I'll give her my fishin' rod as a present. Mother, but come quickly – place me… in my… boat…'

He was buried in the old churchyard of Tullynakill.

WARRENPOINT

Warrenpoint, like Rostrevor, has a spectacular situation with the Cooley Mountains to the southern side of Carlingford Lough and the Mourne Mountains towards the north-east. It's a pleasant place to visit with a lovely tree-lined promenade, and it's interesting watching shipping rounds the docks. There's a ferry that connects Warrenpoint with Omeath in the Irish Free State.

During and after the Second World War, 'Mystery Tours' ran from Belfast to Warrenpoint. 'Mystery Tour' was a bit of a misnomer because everyone knew the bus was going to Warrenpoint and there'd be sufficient time to travel across to Omeath and do a bit of 'smuggling'! Food was rationed in Northern Ireland during and after the war. Sugar, eggs, meat and other items that were in short supply in Northern Ireland but were plentiful across the border as the 'South' remained neutral throughout the war. I have been told the 'smuggling' was a two-way process because tea was plentiful in the North but in short supply in the South.

4

ST PATRICK

We know a lot about St Patrick because two letters, written by him, have survived, namely his 'Confession' and his 'Letter to Coroticus'.

In his 'Confession' St Patrick says he was the son of a wealthy Roman Christian family, who lived in Britain at a place called Bannavem Taburniae. Unfortunately, nobody is entirely certain where that was! Recent archaeological finds make it likely to have been a small settlement called Banna, near Birdoswald Roman Fort, on Hadrian's Wall, 15 miles from Carlisle (Luguvalium).

St Patrick's grandfather was a devout Christian. His father, Calpurnius, was a deacon in the church and a politician. It's impossible to tell if his beliefs were those of a sincere Christian or if they were motivated by politics. In those days it was a 'posh' thing to be a Christian and an active member of the church. It also helped in business dealings.

When St Patrick was 15 years of age and his parents were away from home his house was raided by a bunch of pirates, who captured people and sold them as slaves. They killed the old and infirm. There was no point in allowing anyone who couldn't do a hard day's work to survive – that would have been uneconomic. Such people would just eat food, be difficult to sell, and not contribute to the household. They kidnapped those who looked strong enough to make valuable slaves. The young Patrick and his sister, Lupita, must have appeared strong and healthy because they survived the raid. Patrick was sold to a man called Milchiu, who lived on Slemish Mountain, while his sister was sold as a handmaiden to a family who lived in County Louth.

According to the book *One Thousand and One Irish Saints*, Lupita also became a saint and she was found in the bed of her nephew, St Mel. He was at confession and she said she'd climbed into his bed to gain sanity from the sheets! She got away with that and moved to Armagh, where she became a prostitute. Eventually she annoyed St Patrick by sleeping with St Colman, a saint he didn't like! St Patrick was so enraged that he took his chariot and killed her by running it three times over her body.

I'm only gaining sanity from his sheets. Honest!
(Illustration by Hector McDonnell)

He held confession for her as her soul entered heaven. That's a strange tale when viewed through today's eyes. It was probably invented to enhance St Patrick's reputation but instead it maligns him. There's no evidence he ever had a horse, never mind a chariot. He travelled on foot.

Patrick was a nominal Christian until he hit 'the road to Damascus' on a freezing cold day on Slemish Mountain. He couldn't find all his animals and was terrified. He knew slaves were severely beaten when they lost animals. He fell to his knees and prayed as he'd never prayed before. He told God how frightened he felt, how he was miserable in this strange land and how he hated being a slave. His prayer resulted in a tremendous feeling of peace. He found his animals and stayed out of trouble. After that he often went out in freezing weather to pray. He felt very close to Jesus in those type of conditions. At first the other slaves thought he was stark staring mad but gradually his belief and behaviour impressed them and many of them converted to Christianity.

After six years of slavery Patrick heard God telling him to escape. He must have felt he was going crazy because in those days slaves didn't dare escape, it was too risky. There was nowhere to go as Ireland is a small country. Communities were small and everyone knew everyone else. Strangers were unwelcome and slaves easily identified because they were dressed differently from the general population. A runaway slave would have stuck out like a sore thumb. Escaped slaves were returned to their owners and tortured to death as a warning to the others.

Eventually Patrick became convinced that God really did want him to escape as His voice kept saying, 'Do not be afraid. I will be with you every step of the way.' He walked 200 miles to the coast.

Slemish Mountain is only a few miles from County Antrim's coast so Patrick must have walked inland. Croagh Patrick in County Mayo is about 200 miles from Slemish so perhaps that explains the close connection between St Patrick and County Mayo? He kept out of sight by travelling during the hours of darkness and fed off the land. Eventually he came to the sea and hid in a shepherd's hut until God told him his ship was ready. He looked out and saw a ship in the harbour so he went and asked the captain for a job. He must have been very disappointed when the captain said 'No way!' He turned on his heel and began to walk away but the captain had a change of heart and shouted after him, 'Could you look after our dogs?' Patrick said he could and was told to come on board.

The ship set sail and a terrible storm blew up. Patrick and the sailors were shipwrecked on a barren, uninhabited land. They walked and walked until they could go no further and some of the sailors began to fall by the wayside. The captain flew into a rage and yelled at Patrick, 'I shouldn't have allowed you to come on board! You've brought a curse on us. We've been shipwrecked and are going to die of starvation!' St Patrick fell to his knees and prayed for food and a herd of pigs appeared. The sailors caught, killed and cooked them. Everybody had enough to eat. St Patrick's life was saved and the sailors were able to go back and rescue their companions who'd fallen by the wayside.

Nobody knows where St Patrick went after the shipwreck. All that is known is that he trained as a clergyman and eventually managed to return home to Bannavem Taburniae, where he was reunited with his parents. They must have been astonished to see him. Slaves never escaped, never mind returned home!

St Patrick wrote in his 'Confession' that he was 'a miserable sinner' who was uneducated and who had committed a 'terrible sin' in his youth. He was haunted with guilt by whatever that was. Eventually his best friend persuaded him to confess, to get it off his chest, so to speak, and to forget about it. St Patrick trusted his friend and wept as he narrated what he'd done. He found confessing a relief. Later, when he believed God wanted him go back to Ireland and tell the inhabitants about Jesus, becoming a bishop was a necessary qualification. When he applied to be consecrated his friend proved false, broke his promise and told the church hierarchy about Patrick's 'terrible sin'. As a result, it was decided that Patrick was not a suitable candidate. Patrick was very persistent so he sat down and wrote his 'Confession' to persuade them they should grant his wish. He said he was motivated by a strong desire to tell the Irish about the love of God and described himself in the following words quoted from his 'Confession':

> I, Patrick, a sinner, a most simple countryman, the least of all the faithful and most contemptible to many ...

He explained his motivation by writing:

> In a vision of the night I saw a man whose name was Victorious coming as if from Ireland with innumerable letters ... and they were crying as if with one voice: 'We beg you, holy youth, that you shall come and walk again among us'. And I was stung intensely in my heart ...

He was very persistent so the church hierarchy probably got fed up saying 'No' and granted his wish. It's likely they thought working as a missionary in Ireland would solve their problem because he'd be murdered. At that time, Ireland was a very dangerous place. Its inhabitants had a nasty habit of killing strangers on sight and stealing their possessions.

St Patrick began his missionary work in County Down. He and some of his followers landed where the River Slaney runs into Strangford Lough, near where the village of Strangford is situated today. They hid their boat, began walking inland and were spotted by a local shepherd boy. He told his master, a Chieftain called Dichu, who had a huge ferocious dog, probably an Irish wolfhound, that was trained to kill strangers on sight. Dichu walked towards St Patrick and released his hound, fully expecting the saint to be torn to shreds. The animal charged towards Patrick then licked his hand and lay meekly down at his feet. Dichu was astonished. St Patrick said, 'Jesus looks after me. Nothing can hurt me. God is love and I have come to Ireland to tell you about Him and His son, Jesus. They love you. They love everybody.'

Dichu was impressed by what St Patrick said and gave him his barn. That meant the saint had somewhere to hold

Fido! Will ye stop yer slabbering!

church meetings and the barn developed into his first church. (*Saul* is the Irish word for 'barn'.) Dichu didn't become a Christian, although his wife did.

The present church at Saul was built in 1933 and replaced an older one, the ruins of which may be seen in the churchyard. It's beautiful, very simple, in a stunning setting, always open and well worth a visit. It's signposted on the road between Downpatrick and Strangford. The churchyard contains the ruined remains of an older church, with small worn headstones dating back to Celtic times. The original church would have been made of wood and would have looked like an upturned boat. Obviously wooden buildings don't last as long as those made of stone and even stone ones decay over time and need to be replaced.

St Patrick lived to be an old man and is thought to have died in Raholp, attended by the clergy of St Tassach's Church. Tradition says his friends couldn't decide where he should be buried. Some thought he should be laid to rest in the church he founded on the Hill of Down, while others favoured his church in Armagh. Eventually they placed his body on a slipe (a primitive cart, without wheels and shaped like a sleigh) and harnessed it to a team of oxen. They agreed that wherever the oxen stopped was where St Patrick should be buried. The oxen stopped near the top of the Hill of Down and he was buried in the grounds of what is now Downpatrick Cathedral. The oral tradition states St Patrick's grave also contains the bodies of St Bridget and St Columba. A large rock was placed on it by Belfast Naturalists' Field Club in 1900.

Down Cathedral, situated on the Hill of Down, is well worth a visit. It incorporates parts of a Benedictine monastery, built in 1183. Two small crosses, dating back to the twelfth century, are incorporated into its walls. Building sculpture into walls was once a common practice. It was thought to be a good way to ensure their survival.

The cathedral incorporates the structures of an older church, which had fallen into a terrible state of disrepair and stood, a noble ruin, roofless and derelict for many years. It was eventually renovated between the years 1789 and 1812. Today it's a beautiful building with box pews and fine stained-glass windows. Entrance is free and, to help with the upkeep of such an ancient building, it has an unobtrusive, excellent tourist shop.

Churches are not the only places associated with St Patrick. He is said to have blessed many wells throughout the country, including Struell Wells. They're situated a few miles from Downpatrick Cathedral. (If you're in Downpatrick travel along Edward Street to the Ardglass Road and look for the Struell Road, which is on the left side and travel along it. The wells are signposted. Entrance is free.) The site contains the ruins of a church, two wells and the remains of two bathing houses. The water is said to have healing properties and the site was once used as a place of pilgrimage.

There's an old folk tale saying St Patrick was attempting to sleep beside the Struell stream when water from it splashed his beard and surplice. Any normal saint would have cursed the waters but he was not an ordinary saint! He blessed them, thus giving them healing properties. (There are tales saying he cursed a few other places, such as the River Duff, which he emptied of fish because the locals refused to give him any.)

Protective structures have been placed around Struell Wells. Two bathhouses and a church were also built on the site.

Originally the structures were made of woven branches, which were eventually replaced by buildings built of stone. One of the wells is reputed to cure bad backs. My back's fine so I've never used its waters. The other well is said to cure deteriorating eyesight. I once washed my eyes in it and was convinced my sight did improve. Later I learnt that while bathing the eyes one should be praying for spiritual sight and I didn't do that. I just wanted to avoid wearing glasses so I could see more clearly to read. I suspect thinking my sight improved was a placebo effect. Or perhaps increasing light made seeing easier as winter turned into spring? I ended up needing glasses about a year later.

There are two ruined bathhouses on the site now, one for men and one for women. The oral history records that originally there was only one bathhouse. Men and women stripped naked and sat together taking the healing waters. At a later date another house was built and the sexes were separated.

I tested the temperature of the water rushing into the women's bathhouse. It was freezing! I was glad not to be living in the past and on a pilgrimage. Putting my hand in the water was bad enough, never mind the whole of my body being exposed, naked, to Irish weather by sitting on stone-cold seats in freezing water! That's the strange thing about water in holy wells. The temperature deviates from that found in normal wells. It's either warmer or colder, or occasionally, as in the case of St Patrick's Holy Well in Belcoo, County Fermanagh, it's warm in winter and cold in summer!

As well as creating holy wells, St Patrick established major churches in Bangor, Newry, Dromore, Armagh, and Down Cathedral, which is in Downpatrick and bears his name. His establishment in Bangor became famous for the excellence of the education provided here. It attracted scholars from throughout the then known world (see Chapter 2).

St Patrick is said to have planted a yew tree at the land end of Carlingford Lough in Newry (see Chapter 2), thus giving the city its name, and Armagh developed into the ecclesiastical centre of Ireland. Most of his missionary work was done in the north of Ireland but surprisingly folklore states he never visited the Kingdom of Mourne. He just travelled around the foothills and is said to have looked along the path leading round the shore where the Mountains of Mourne sweep down to the sea, thrown his brogue along it and said, 'May peace reign in their region.' Although St Patrick never visited the Mournes, his followers founded five churches near the shoreline.

St Patrick's main route from Bangor to Armagh was through Downpatrick, Castlewellan, Newry and on to Armagh, but sometimes he travelled from Castlewellan to Seapatrick, Tullylish and on to Armagh.

Banbridge didn't exist in those days and Seapatrick was a convenient place to spend a night, so he founded a church there.

Local oral tradition says Seapatrick, now on the outskirts of Banbridge, was founded by the saint himself. It's a long way from the sea, so why is the word 'sea' incorporated in its name? Words and spellings change over time so if a word in the past, or a name, bears any resemblance to what we recognise today that's probably what it means. 'Sea' sounds the same as 'See', which is the earliest symbol of a bishop's authority. It usually corresponds to a diocese.

Seapatrick is part of the Diocese of Down and Dromore, one of the two largest dioceses belonging to the Church of Ireland. It stretches from County Down into County Armagh. It contains 477 parishes, 2 cathedrals (Downpatrick and Armagh), 111 churches, 1,800 clergy, 64,500 people and it shares Belfast Cathedral with the Diocese of Conor.

St Patrick's church at Seapatrick is known locally as the 'Wee Church' to differentiate it from Banbridge's other Anglican church, Holy Trinity, known as the 'Big Church'. The two churches share clergymen and events.

Banbridge expanded during the late eighteenth and early nineteenth century after a new bridge was built over the River Bann. It had far-reaching consequences as it caused the route of the old coach road to be diverted across the new bridge over the River Bann rather than use the ford at Ballykeel. As a result, the settlement called Ballyvalley became known as Banbridge (see Chapter 3).

The focus of the town changed so the Anglican Church decided to move premises and build a new church in what is now known as Church Square. They believed the move would attract extra trade, so to speak. Some people who attended the 'Wee Church' were not pleased. They refused to move and a compromise was reached. In 1880 in Seapatrick the nearby disused schoolhouse was refurbished and dedicated to St Patrick. St Patrick's church was consecrated for worship in 1882 and services have been held there ever since. Holy Trinity is the name of the 'new church'. Members of the congregation can choose which church they attend.

The 'Wee Church' has two bells, a small one on a bell tower and a large one at the side. It is the large bell that is tolled manually each Sunday, at present by Rodney Mitchell. It is said a bell has been rung every Sunday on the site since St Patrick walked the earth (except during times of war).

Locally there was great consternation when planning permission was given to build houses adjacent to the site. It was thought that the occupants would object to the sound of the bell. As a result, the leases of the houses state occupants have no right to restrict the sound of a bell that has rung more or less continuously for more than 1,700 years.

There's an interesting well-like structure beside the 'Wee Church'. According to local oral history, it was one of the reasons St Patrick founded his church there. The late local historian, Horace Rea, decided to take the tradition seriously and arranged for an expert water diviner to visit the site. He discovered a buried well! The congregation was delighted and the well was uncovered. Unfortunately, Health and Safety worried in case anyone should fall in and insisted it was covered up again. The present well-like structure marks the spot.

The 'Big Church' was dedicated to the Holy Trinity and consecrated on 7 November 1837. It was enlarged in 1887 when the roof was raised 6ft and transepts were added.

Over a period of time the spire became crooked. The then Rector, Venerable Archdeacon John Scott, became concerned because stones began falling off the roof. He spent so much time climbing around it he became known as 'the fiddler on the roof'. He obtained a professional survey, which declared the spire was in a perilous state and needed to be rebuilt at a cost of approximately £500,000. The church is a Grade B listed building. Heritage Lottery Funding was sought, and awarded, and the congregation was given the mammoth task of raising the remaining £250,000. In the interim a canopy was built around the main door so building blocks would fall on it rather than parishioners attending church.

Money was raised by the usual methods of running sales, coffee mornings and so on. The community living in Banbridge contributed generously, regardless of the church they attended. Catholics and Protestant and those of no religion helped to restore the spire. In addition, Captain Geoffrey Walmsley was sponsored to sit in a bath of beans in the middle of the town while members of the congregation took it in turns to make a street collection. The Reverend Mark Greenstreet gamely ran the Belfast Marathon and was sponsored to do so. The money was raised within eleven months.

St Patrick appears to have been a gentle, affable man but it was possible to make him lose his temper. When Coroticus kidnapped some of his converts, killed the elderly ones and sold the young ones as slaves, he wrote that he hoped 'the riches which he [Coroticus] has unjustly gathered will be vomited from his belly ... the angel of death will hand him over to be crushed by the anger of dragons ... he will be killed with the viper's tongue and an unquenchable fire will consume him'. Stirring words indeed! I must confess when I read them I warmed to him. His reaction is very human. Folklore says he got his revenge on Coroticus by turning him into a fox!

St Patrick appears to have been a godly man, who did a lot of good and was greatly loved and respected. Unfortunately, during the seventh century two monks, Tíerechán and Muirchu, decided to enhance St Patrick's reputation by writing his life

May the riches he has unjustly gathered be vomited from his belly, may he be killed with the viper's tongue, may an unquenchable fire consume him.

story. Until then St Patrick was a simple sincere man who popularised Christianity.

After Tíerechán and Muirchu had finished with him he passed into folklore looking more like a wizard, an unbelievable character credited with all sorts of magic powers. For instance, it is said he caused two brothers who were fighting over the ownership of a piece of land to freeze. He told them firmly they wouldn't be able to move unless they gave the land to a church. Another unbelievable tale is that he once asked a dead pagan man why he'd a cross over his grave. The dead man replied it had been put there by mistake. He didn't want it so St Patrick removed it and set it over the right grave. That was a clever trick because the saint had been dead for several hundred years!

Another ridiculous story tells how a local chieftain's subjects were sickening and dying. He said to St Patrick: 'There's a poisonous yellow fog hanging over the River Lagan. It stinks and it's killing my people. Men, women and children perish whenever they go near the river to collect water. Collecting water's so dangerous we've none to drink, or to use in cooking or to keep ourselves clean. Can you do anything? We'd hate to leave our village although I have told everyone to be prepared to do so.'

St Patrick asked, 'Do you think a dead animal fell into the waters and tainted them?'

'Oh no! It's much more serious than that. I believe the river is inhabited by a demon.'

St Patrick walked over the hill towards the river. A terrible acrid stench filled the air and a thin yellow gauze of mist stretched over the countryside. He began to choke and shouted, 'Jesus protect me!'

The fog became denser. St Patrick could hardly see his hand in front of him. The grass around his feet turned black. He reached the riverbank. The water was covered in a thick yellowish scum with an oily rainbow swirling across its surface. He thought, 'I'll have to burn my robes and sandals. They'll be covered by deadly poison. The trouble must be caused by a Formorian king, who has turned into a devil.' (The Formors were the people who lived in Ireland before the Tuatha De Danann invaded the country and drove them away. A few are said to have escaped and hidden themselves in streams and wells.)

St Patrick prayed, 'Dear Lord, deliver me from this evil demon.' The water stirred and bubbled. The stench was unbelievable. The saint staggered backwards and almost fell on the poisoned grass. He gasped, raised his voice and shouted, 'Satanic devil! Be gone in the name of Jesus.'

A ghastly scaled head broke the surface of the fetid water. Its flat yellow eyes with their slit-like pupils stared unblinkingly at him. The creature was twice as tall as a man and looked like a cross between a man and an evil serpent. It was covered in scales that leaked a disgusting yellow substance. Its head jutted forward, its mouth opened and St Patrick could see its forked tongue and rows of sharp, triangular teeth. Its tail lashed the water to a foam and its long thin arms stretched towards him.

St Patrick shouted, 'Spawn of Satan I banish you in the name of the one true God, the Lord Jesus Christ. In the name of the Father, the Son and the Holy Spirit, be gone!'

The creature howled and spat filthy yellow liquid at the saint, who raised his hand and made the sign of the cross. The water burst into flame and exploded like a bomb. The blast lifted St Patrick off his feet and threw him onto the blackened grass. The Formor howled with pain. Liquid fire shot from every scale as it melted into the boiling river waters.

That's the type of story St Patrick's biographers wrote with the intention of enhancing his reputation. Unfortunately, they turned him into an unbelievable character and obscured his tremendous achievement. He became the Patron Saint of Ireland and turned what was basically a pagan country into a Christian one. He was a good, simple, sincere man, who despite the dangers of having to work in a hostile environment, laid the foundation of Ireland's reputation as a land of saints and scholars.

5

FAMOUS PEOPLE, ROGUES AND VAGABONDS

SIR HANS SLOAN, FOUNDER OF THE BRITISH MUSEUM

Hans Sloan (1660–1753) was born in Killyleagh. He studied medicine in France at Paris and Montpellier before graduating at the University of Orange in 1683.

Between the years 1687 and 1689 he was physician to the governor of Jamaica. This mustn't have been an arduous job because he was able to collect 800 new specimens of Jamaican plants. He published a catalogue of them, in Latin, in 1696.

Sir Hans Sloan is noted for writing two monumental works, *A Voyage to the Islands of Madeira, Jamaica etc.*, and *The Natural History of Jamaica*, published in two volumes in 1707 and in 1725.

Just think – the founder of the British Museum was yer man from Killyleagh!

He was responsible for introducing drinking chocolate to Britain and he gained an excellent reputation as a physician, resulting in his appointment as physician to George II in 1716. He was awarded a baronetcy, was honoured by many foreign academies of science and in 1727 became President of the Royal Society. By the time of his death in 1753 he had a library of 3,500 manuscripts, 50,000 books and many cabinets containing numerous curiosities and specimens. He made a bargain with the British Museum in which they agreed to pay his family £20,000 if he bequeathed his collection to them. The museum was delighted to take possession of a collection at a price that was very much below its market value. It formed the nucleus of the British Museum, which opened its doors to the public in 1753.

PATRICK BRONTË, FATHER OF THE BRONTË SISTERS

The story of the famous Brontë sisters ends in Haworth in Yorkshire, but it begins in County Down, where their father, Revd Patrick Brontë, was born of humble farming stock. His parents, Hugh Brunty and Alice McCrory, married in Magerally Church in 1776. The officiating clergyman said she was the most beautiful bride he had ever seen.

The young couple started married life by living with Alice's brother until they found a two-bedroomed cottage nearby. They used one room as a bedroom and parlour, the other as a corn kiln, kitchen and reception room.

Patrick was born on St Patrick's Day 1777. Over time the family name turned to Bronte and eventually to Brontë. There are two theories regarding the acquisition of the 'ë', namely that when he was entering Cambridge the Registrar made a mistake. Patrick didn't correct the spelling error because he thought it looked elegant. The other theory is that Patrick changed his name because he was an admirer of Lord Nelson, who'd been awarded the Duchy of Brontë in Sicily by King Ferdinand III of Italy in recognition of his services during the

Napoleonic Wars. Sicilians are very proud of their Brontë connection. (There is a Brontë region in Sicily on the northern slopes of Mount Etna.)

Patrick's father, Hugh Brunty, was a gifted storyteller who held his family and neighbours enthralled. Patrick inherited his father's gift and influenced his daughters' stories.

Patrick Brontë's County Down upbringing was evident throughout his life. For instance, his mother was an expert spinner. She obtained wool from her brother's sheep and turned it into woollen clothes. Patrick had a dread of wearing garments made of anything other than wool. He said if he was dressed in cotton he'd catch his death of cold! He taught himself to weave and once he'd acquired that skill his family were self-sufficient regarding clothing.

Patrick's first job was as a weaver. He inherited a love of learning from his parents, which proved deleterious to his skills as a weaver because he used to weave with a book propped up on the loom in front of him. As a result, he made mistakes and got the sack. He got another job, this time as a teacher at Glascar School. Unfortunately, he fell in love with one of his pupils and was dismissed. That wasn't as bad as it sounds because there was very little difference in their ages. After that he was very lucky to obtain a post at Drumballyroney School, where he was taken under the wing of the rector, the Revd Thomas Tighe, who encouraged him to apply for a university education. As a result, he won a scholarship to attend St John's College, Cambridge. He obtained his degree, was ordained as a clergyman and the rest is history!

Patrick Brontë is said to have preached his first sermon in Drumballyroney Church. The churchyard contains the Brontë family grave. If you want to visit the grave go behind the church and keep close to the church wall. The grave is clearly marked near the hedge close to the church wall.

ERNEST SINTON WALTON
(1903–1995), PHYSICIST

Ernest Walton (1903–1995) was born in Abbeyside, Dungarvan, County Waterford, the son of a Methodist minister. The Methodist Church moves clergymen approximately every five years. As a result, the young Ernest came with his family to live in Banbridge when his father was the incumbent of Banbridge Methodist Church. He, in common with many sons of Methodist ministers, became a border at the Methodist College Belfast, where he excelled in science and mathematics.

Professor Walton was the first scientist to observe artificial splitting of the atom. His discovery came as a result of experimental procedures he and his partner, John Cockcroft, designed in the early 1930s at Cambridge University. As a result, they were awarded a Nobel Peace Prize in 1951.

I too attended the Methodist College and was in the same form as Ernest's daughter, Marion. She told me that her father was horrified by the destruction of Nagasaki and Hiroshima caused by further development of his research. He was a deeply religious man who once stated, 'One way to learn the mind of the Creator is to study His Creation … A refusal to use our intelligence honestly is an act of contempt for Him who gave us that intelligence.' He left Cambridge and became a lecturer in Trinity College, Dublin, where he gained an excellent reputation as a brilliant lecturer, with the ability to make complex ideas easily understood.

DOLLY MUNROE, FAMOUS BEAUTY
FROM LAURENCETOWN

Dorothea Munroe (1754–1793), known as Dolly, was so beautiful that she inspired poets, including Oliver Goldsmith, who mentioned her in his poem 'The Haunch of Venison':

Of the breast and the neck I still had to dispose,
'Twas the breast and the neck that would rival Munroe's.

Dolly Munroe, daughter of a linen merchant, was born in Rosehill, a mansion at Laurencetown. It has since been knocked down and replaced by a housing estate of the same name. She was a beautiful, sweet-natured little girl, who had a very sheltered childhood. Her life was so quiet she once wrote to a friend describing the excitement she had felt when taken, by a maid, on a shopping expedition to Banbridge. She was left to amuse herself in the graveyard of the Anglican church at Seapatrick, about a mile from the town. (A vault to the left of the gate of belongs to the Munroe family.)

In 1745 Dolly's aunt, Frances Munroe, married Viscount Loftus of Ely, who had a castle at Rathfarnham and a townhouse in Hume Street, Dublin. Frances was fond of Dolly so, when she was 18, she brought her to Dublin.

Dolly caused a sensation! She was so beautiful and became so popular she had to take her early morning walk at 6 a.m. to avoid the crowds surrounding her aunt's house! Newspapers reported her every movement and printed poems and articles about her. Many painters captured her beauty and there are two portraits in the Irish National Gallery in Dublin.

In 1775 Dolly married Mr William Richardson of Richhill. She had a happy marriage. The couple travelled widely and had a villa in Italy. Unfortunately, they had no children. Dolly died in 1793 and was buried in her husband's family grave in Richhill.

FRANCIS CROZIER, EXPLORER

Francis Crozier (1796–1848) is credited with finding the Northwest Passage around Canada. He was second in command to Sir John Franklin when they set sail on an expedition to discover a passage around the North Pole in 1845. They never returned.

In 1859 an expedition discovered, from messages found in the region, that the two ships, *Erebus* and *Terror*, had become locked in ice and that Franklin died on 11 June 1847 and Crozier took charge of the expedition.

In April 1848, Captain Francis Crozier decided to abandon his ship, the *Terror*, and attempted to lead the remaining survivors across the ice to safety. All that is known is scraps of information, in steel tubes, left along the way by members of the crew and from facts gleaned from Inuits by another expedition, led by Captain James Clinton, that set out for the Arctic in 1885. Inuits told him white men had left their ships and died of starvation.

According to the late Dr Maurna Crozier, wife of the late Julien Crozier, it's amazing how many people claim direct descent from Francis Crozier. That's a clever trick as he never married and had no offspring! (Maurna's husband was descended from one of Crozier's brothers.)

In 2014 a Canadian expedition discovered the *Erebus*, using sonar, lying on the seabed in Queen Maud Gulf, that's 160km to the south of the point where she and *Terror* had been abandoned. Nobody knows how it got there, but it's clear Francis Crozier did discover the Northwest Passage although he didn't live to tell the tale.

PROFESSOR FRANK PANTRIDGE, INVENTOR OF THE PROTABLE DEFIBRILLATOR

Frank Pantridge (1916–2004) was born outside Hillsborough, on a farm overlooking the Maze Racecourse and Government House.

He was educated at Downshire Primary School in Hillsborough, Friend's School, Lisburn and Queen's University Belfast. He qualified as a doctor and was serving an internship in the Royal Victoria Hospital (RVH) when the Second World War broke out. He joined up and was posted to the Far East. He was a medical officer with an infantry battalion before and during the Japanese invasion of Malaya, during which time he won an immediate award of the Military Cross in the field. The *London Gazette* printed the following citation:

During the operations in Johore and Singapore … as medical officer attached to the 2/Gordons, this officer worked unceasingly under the most adverse conditions of continuous bombing and shelling and was an inspiring example to all with whom he came in contact. He was absolutely cool under the heaviest fire and completely regardless of his own personal safety at all times.

Dr Pantridge was taken prisoner and survived working on the notorious Siam–Burma railway and the 'death camp' at Tanbaya in Burma. When he was liberated he weighed less than 5 stone. The lower part of his body was bloated with the dropsy and beriberi, while the upper half was emaciated, skin and bones. His friend, Dr Tom Milliken, said, 'He was a physical wreck but his spirit was obviously unbroken. The eyes said it was indestructible.'

On his return to what he referred to as 'God's own country' Dr Pantridge continued his internship in RVH and undertook research. He caused a lot of consternation when he brought pigs into the hospital because he was investigating the mechanism of sudden death from beriberi! He said his research had little value but it did win him a scholarship to work with Frank Wilson, the world authority on electrocardiography. On his return he introduced mitral valvotomy to surgeons in RVH and eventually established the Regional Medical Cardiology Centre.

In the mid-1960s coronary heart disease had reached enormous proportions and was striking younger people. Dr Pantridge turned his attention to coronary attack and sudden death. By the mid-1950s it had been shown to be due to the heart beating in a disorganised fashion and that it could be cured by giving the heart an electric shock. Dr Pantridge said hospital care units were useless when treating coronary patients because two-thirds of the deaths occurred within an hour of the onset of an attack, that is before the patient reached hospital. He pointed out that if a dead patient arrives at a coronary care unit it's too late to help! He decided to bring the hospital to the patient. He got an old ambulance and installed an ordinary hospital defibrillator inside, with an adapted car battery and all the drugs and equipment normally present in a coronary care unit. Hospital personnel were trained. A rota was formed of junior doctors and nurses and he'd a special telephone line installed in the coronary care unit to summon help wherever it was needed. Unfortunately, there was stiff opposition to heart-ambulances at home, but the idea caught on in America and the rest is history.

Dr Pantridge's goal was to develop a defibrillator that was compact and light enough to be truly portable. He made several attempts before that was achieved.

Local historian Norman Kerr has an interesting museum at Laurencetown containing the second defibrillator designed by Dr Pantridge. It's powered by a car battery and is too cumbersome to be truly portable. Developments in modern technology solved the difficulty of supplying power so today defibrillators, complete with instructions, are widely available.

Frank Pantridge died at the age of 88 and is buried in Hillsborough Parish Church's graveyard. (His grave is straight down the main path on the left-hand corner formed by the first side path joining the main path.)

NED KELLY, AUSTRALIAN FOLK HERO

In 1909 the Australian newspaper *Adelaide Advertiser* printed a story about the ancestral home of Australian folk hero Ned Kelly, in Townsend Street, Banbridge, being demolished. The oral history of Banbridge states that the Kelly family lived in a cul-de-sac called Brick Lane, off Townsend Street.

Ned Kelly's father, John Kelly (known as Red Kelly), was baptised on 20 February 1820 in Moyglass Church in the parish of Killenaule in County Tipperary, which is a long way from Banbridge, County Down! The Kelly family were ruffians, who made frequent appearances before the local courts. They probably moved to Banbridge to avoid trouble. Communications in the early nineteenth century were poor so the best way to escape punishment was to disappear to another part of the country!

Ye're kidding! Ned Kelly's family can't have lived for a time in Brick Lane off Townsend Street!

Eventually Red Kelly was caught, tried and sentenced to be deported to Australia for stealing two pigs.

After his deportation, Red Kelly went gold prospecting and earned enough money to buy a small freehold farm in Victoria, where the family gained a reputation for cattle rustling. Ned Kelly was born in 1854.

In 1865, Red Kelly was jailed for stealing and skinning a calf. Conditions in jails were terrible. He became ill and died soon after he was released.

The Kellys were a close family, so when Ah Fook, a Chinese pig farmer, abused Ned's sister Annie, Ned defended her. Ah Fook gave him a good beating and took him to court for assaulting him! Thankfully Ned wasn't convicted.

After that Ned Kelly had several brushes with the law, including the bizarre offence of riding a policeman like a horse!

Serious trouble occurred in 1878 when Alexander Fitzpatrick went to the Kelly homestead to arrest Ned's younger brother, Dan. Ned's mother, Ellen, hit the constable on the head with a shovel and he said his wrist had been injured when Ned shot him three times. Fitzpatrick was treated by a doctor, who didn't believe the injury was caused by gunshot wounds. Historians think Fitzpatrick was an unreliable witness because, three years previously, he'd lost his job in the police force. He'd been found guilty of perjury and drunkenness. But that didn't help either

Ned or his brother Dan. They became outlaws and went on the run, along with their friends Steve Hart and Joe Byrne. As the police closed in, the gang attempted to steal weapons from four officers. One of the officers went for his gun and Ned shot him dead.

The Kelly gang committed many crimes before making their last stand against the forces of the law at Glenrowan, when Ned Kelly donned his home-made metal armour. It's become a powerful symbol in Australian art.

Ned was captured, tried and convicted on three counts of murder. On 11 November 1880 he was led from Melbourne Gaol at 5 a.m. and hanged by Elija Upjohn. Contemporary accounts say it was Upjohn's first execution; he was an ugly man with a huge carbuncle on the end of his nose.

Legend records Ned Kelly's last words as 'Such is life'! He remains a prominent figure among Australia's anti-heroes. He's seen by some as a common criminal and by others as symbolising national Irish–Australian resistance to unfair government.

Ned Kelly's torso was thrown into a mass grave at the Old Melbourne Jail. His head was removed and handed to phrenologists to look for evidence of criminal activity by studying its 'bumps'. (Phrenology, the study of skulls to determine a person's character and mental ability, was a popular pseudo-science in the Victorian Age.)

Before DNA testing, bodies in mass graves were difficult to identify because there was no means of saying which set of bones belonged to whom. However, Ned Kelly had been given a special pair of boots as a reward for rescuing a drowning teenager. He wore them during the final stand at Glenrowan, when his boots and sash became splattered by his blood. He was buried with his sash and boots on, so the bones near the boots were presumed to have belonged to him. Samples of blood taken from them were used for DNA testing in 2011. They confirmed the bones found beside his boots in a mass grave at Melbourne's Pentridge Prison really did belong to Ned Kelly. (Bodies from the Old Melbourne Jail's graveyard were reinterred at Pentridge Prison in 1929.)

A head, thought to belong to Ned Kelly, was put on display when the old gaol was turned into a museum in 1971. Unfortunately, it was stolen.

A skull said to belong to Ned Kelly was reported in the *New Zealand Herald on Sunday* on 28 August 2012. It belonged to Anna Hoffman, a 74-year-old New Zealand woman who collected skulls. She said she'd been given Ned's head by a mysterious uniformed man after a family dinner party in 1980. He'd told her to 'wrap it up' and to put it in the bottom of a cupboard. Deb Withers, a spokesman for the Victorian Institute of Forensic Science, said, 'There's a chance that it's Ned's head, although it is a long shot.'

Gina McFarlane, a forensic expert at Auckland University, said she thought the wires sticking out of the skull suggested it had been used as a teaching aid, which made it unlikely to have belonged to Ned Kelly. That begs the question: where is Ned Kelly's head?

Ned's family campaigned to be allowed to give him a proper burial. His last wish was that his remains should lie beside his mother in the family plot at Gretna. In January 2013 his wish was granted and Joanne Griffiths, the great-granddaughter of Kelly's sister Kate, said, 'We've made a real effort to ensure that he's safe and surrounded by family and friends. That's what he wanted.'

AMY CARMICHAEL, SELFLESS SERVANT OF INDIA

Amy Carmichael (1867–1971) didn't like the colour of her eyes. She wanted blue eyes, not brown ones, but those brown eyes were very useful when she worked as a missionary in India because they enabled her to disguise herself and pass as a native by using coffee to dye her skin brown and dressing in Indian clothing.

Amy was born in Millisle, the eldest of Catherine Wilson and David Carmichael's seven children. Her family were rich

Yon Amy Carmichael
was a great wee worker.

Presbyterian flour mill owners. Her father died in 1885 and
the family found themselves in reduced circumstances. They
moved to Belfast, where Amy became upset by the plight of
the poor. At that time Belfast was the greatest centre of the
linen industry in the world. Mill owners became rich while
the mill workers were poverty-stricken, working in dangerous,
unhealthy conditions with no compensation if they were
injured, or killed, at work.

Mill girls couldn't afford coats, so they wrapped themselves
in shawls and became known as 'shawlies'. Amy was heart sorry
for the them and, with the help of two donations (£500 from
Miss Kate Mitchell and a plot of land from a mill owner) she
opened the Welcome Hall in Cambrai Street, off the Shankill
Road, in the mid-1880s to help them. Invitations were sent out
that read 'Come one and all to the Welcome Hall – come in your
working clothes'.

Eventually Amy became convinced that God wanted her
to become a missionary. She joined the Anglican Church's
Missionary Society and was sent to work as a missionary

in Japan and Ceylon (now Sri Lanka). In the mid-1890s she moved to the Tinnevelly district of India, where she became an itinerant missionary.

In 1890 Amy settled in Dohnavur, 30 miles from the southern tip of India. Many children were forced to work as prostitutes in Hindu temples and she began rescuing them. Her organisation was called the Dohnavur Fellowship. Its members were sensitive to Indian culture so they wore Indian dress and the children were given Indian names. Amy often disguised herself as a native and travelled long distances to rescue a child. She rescued, cared for and educated hundreds of children, and wrote, 'One can give without loving, but one cannot love without giving.' There is no doubt she loved her charges and they loved her.

Amy's work in India earned the sincere admiration of Queen Mary, the wife of King George V.

In 1916 Amy founded 'Sisters of the Common Life', a spiritual support group. In 1918 she was awarded the Kaisar-i-Hind medal for service to India. In 1925 there was an attempted takeover, so she broke all ties with missionary societies and opened a hospital in 1929.

In 1931 Amy was injured by a fall and left bedridden for most of her remaining life. She was 83 when she died on 18 January 1951. She was buried at Dohnavur.

Amy was a modest woman who said she didn't want a headstone, so 'her' children put a birdbath on top of her grave. It is inscribed with a single word, 'Amma' (the Tamil word for mother).

Amy was a prolific writer – thirty of her books are still available on Goodreads – but her most impressive legacy is the work at Dohnavur Fellowship, which is still continuing today more than sixty years after her death.

The Ulster History Circle has two blue plaques to commemorate her life, one on the Welcome Evangelical Church in Cambrai Street off Belfast's Shankill Road and the other at the Baptist Church in Millisle.

MARGARET MORROW BYERS, EDUCATIONALIST

Margaret Morrow Byers (1832–1912) was born in Rathfriland. She married Revd John Myers, a missionary, and the young couple moved to China, where John unfortunately died in 1853.

After her husband's death, Margaret spent some time in New York and became an admirer of the American education system, which made little distinction between the education of boys and that of girls. She brought her young son home and supported herself by teaching in a very traditional school in Cookstown.

Margaret was unhappy in Cookstown because she disagreed with what she was expected to teach and the teaching methods used, so, in 1859, she founded the Ladies Collegiate School in Wellington Place, Belfast. It had a more challenging curriculum than usual for girls at the time. The subjects taught included Natural Science, Latin, Greek, and Modern History, as well as the usual French and needlework. In 1873 she built a new school at Lower Crescent, Belfast. In 1887 the school was renamed Victoria College in honour of the fiftieth anniversary of Queen Victoria's accession to the throne and the old building is still standing. At one time it was threatened with demolition but was saved by a public outcry, was restored, and is now thriving as the Crescent Arts Centre, which has a pleasant coffee shop open to the public.

Victoria College was the first Irish school to offer education for girls up to university examination standards. The success of its pupils influenced the inclusion of girls in the 1878 Irish Intermediate Education Act.

In 1908 Margaret Byers became a member of the senate of the new Queen's University Belfast. She died on 21 February 1912 and was buried in Belfast's City cemetery.

JOHN MITCHEL, POLITICIAN

John Mitchel (1815–1875) was born near Dungiven, County Londonderry, the son of a Presbyterian minister. He trained as a

The British Lion and the Irish Monkey.

solicitor and in 1840 obtained a job with Mr Fraser in Newry, County Down. The firm expanded and opened premises in Banbridge, where John lived and worked for five years and where two of his children were born. His sister ran Banbridge post office.

During the time he was working in Banbridge John became enraged at the plight of subsistence farmers during the Great Famine (1845–1847). He wrote pamphlets and articles attacking what he perceived as the government's inaction. In 1848, he started a journal called *The United Irishman*. His writing caused him to be tried for treason, found guilty, transported to Bermuda, then on to Tasmania. He served fourteen years as a prisoner before escaping and travelling to South Carolina, where he became a supporter of the South during the American Civil War. He thought American slaves were treated better than the poor in Ireland, so slavery should be retained.

John Mitchel returned to Ireland and was elected as a Member of Parliament for Tipperary in 1875. The election was declared invalid because he was a convicted felon and a by-election was called. He stood again and was re-elected with an increased majority. This posed a problem for the government, which was solved when John died of natural causes in 1875. His grave is in Newry.

WILLIAM KENNEDY, THE BLIND PIPER

Towards the end of the eighteenth century, Europe welcomed a wave of cultural and creative activity. The arts, literature and music flourished and a piper, William Kennedy, contributed with enthusiasm.

In 1821 James Wilson wrote a book called *A Biography of the Blind*. It contains an interview with William Kennedy, who was then a very old man.

William was born near Banbridge in 1768 and lost his sight when he was 4 years of age. It was customary to send blind children to train as musicians so that they could earn a living. When he was 13 he was sent to Mr Moorehead in Armagh to learn to play the fiddle. William made good progress and stayed there for over a year. He lodged with a cabinet-maker who taught him how to use tools and make furniture.

William came back home and used his new skills to make and sell furniture. He bought an old dilapidated set of Irish Uilleann pipes with some of the money he'd earned. This type of musical instrument gets its name from the Irish word *uilleann*, meaning elbow. It's a type of bagpipe that uses the elbow to expel and suck in air.

William found putting his old pipes back into playing order very difficult but it taught him how they were made. They were a popular instrument, used for social dancing and by Protestant clergymen as a substitute for a church organ.

William's neighbours and friends learnt of his interest in pipes and began bringing broken ones to him to be repaired. He thought about how he could improve the instrument and began making suitable tools. His first set of new improved pipes were built from scratch and completed within nine months. He added keys to the chanter, making it possible to play sharps and flats, extended the range so the instrument could play high E, and added two large keys played with the wrist so that part, or all, of the basses could be opened at will. This was an amazing achievement for someone who was completely blind. He couldn't see black ebony or white ivory but his sense of touch was very sensitive and he used it to tell the difference.

A local clockmaker interested in learning how to play the pipes soon became a close friend. He taught William how to make clocks and William taught him how to make Uillean pipes!

William married in 1793 and spent the next twelve years supporting his wife and family by making all sorts of clocks, repairing pipes, making linen looms and occasionally furniture.

In 1868 the *Armagh Guardian* reported that William said he hated to hear people pitying his parents because they had a blind son so he'd decided to use his other senses to make himself as useful as possible. He believed determination and a sense of duty enabled anybody to do anything. He realised that because he was blind he would need to have several occupations if he wanted to be independent and he was delighted to be able to support his parents in their old age. He said, 'The only thing I ask of God now is health, for as to fortune, He has given me an exhaustless one in my workshop. The blind ones in this world are not they who cannot see the sun but they who cannot see duty.'

William Kennedy's obituary appeared in the *Newry Telegraph* on 11 November 1834:

The late William Kennedy, of Tandragee
Died, at Tandragee on the morning of the 29th October, Mr. William Kennedy, one of the most extraordinary men who have appeared in these latter times. Though totally deprived of sight, he was enabled through his industry, his perseverance and his genius to execute with precision, taste and judgement, various elaborate works of a nature which have required the utmost exertions of well trained artists ... Add to this he was a kindly, industrious, moral and religious

man, an affectionate husband, and, in all respects, an useful and justly esteemed member of society.

Today the Uilleann pipes are kept alive in Banbridge by Brendan Monaghan, who has travelled the world and worked with stars such as Phil Coulter.

AMANDA MCKITTRICK ROS, THE WORLD'S WORST NOVELIST

Anna Margaret McKittrick (1860–1939) was born on 8 December 1860 in Drumaness, near Ballynahinch, County Down, the fourth child of Edward Amlave McKittrick and Eliza Black. Her father was the headmaster of Drumaness High School, near Ballynahinch, County Down.

Anna Margaret considered her name 'too plain' for someone born with what she considered her undeniable talent, so after she was married she renamed herself Amanda Molvina Fitzalan Anna Margaret McClelland McKittrick Ros.

Amanda trained as a teacher and obtained a job in Millbrook School, Larne, County Antrim, where she met the stationmaster, Andy Ross, and married him on 30 August 1887. Part of his attraction must have been his job. Stationmasters occupied a respectable place in local society and Amanda had illusions of grandeur! She wrote:

Love is pleasing, more so money,
Powerful factor – life's best honey,
Super for the gift of God
To a world of sin and fraud.

It was during the years of her marriage to Andy Ross that Amanda self-published the first of her 'great' novels, *Irene Iddesleigh*. She said, 'I don't believe in publishers who wish to butter their bannocks on both sides while they'll hardly allow an author to smell the treacle.' However, she was completely devoid of talent or a sense of humour but her books sold and her fame spread far and wide. King George V was said to have bought twenty-five copies.

Irene Iddesleigh caused a sensation around Ballynahinch, where its unconscious humour was appreciated. Locals spent many amusing evenings reciting passages from it. They sent a copy to a popular humourist, Barry Pain, who wrote a weekly article in a widely distributed paper called *Black and White*. He described Amanda's book as 'a thing that happens once in a million years, a great tragedy, at the price of half a crown'.

Barry Pain's comments upset Amanda, who developed a long-lasting hatred of critics, describing them as 'a bloody blinkers of talent'. She complained there was no reason for anyone to comment on her work 'without being asked to do so'. When she was annoyed, her language was inventive and abusive in the extreme. She took great delight in writing 'poetry', including epitaphs for people she disliked. When Barry Paine died she was delighted and wrote:

> Epitaph suitable for a Critic's Tomb
> My! What a bubbly, vapoury box of vanity!
> A litter of worms, a relic of humanity,
> Once a plaster cast of mud, puff of breath as well
> Before you choose to wander – remember there's a hell!
> So here lies an honest critic and I tell thee what,
> 'Tis a thing for all the world to wonder at!

Amanda loved alliteration. Her fertile imagination invented such descriptions as 'character clipping combination', 'crab clay of corruption', and 'evil minded-snapshot of spleen'. She described Lewis Carroll, author of *Alice in Wonderland*, as a 'drunken cleric in his dotage' and thought the poetry of Keats, Shelley and Wordsworth worthless. She was the only author she admired! She wrote, 'My works are all expressly my own, not a borrowed stroke in one of them. I write as I feel and as I don't feel.'

Clubs were formed in Ballynahinch, Oxford, Cambridge and London by people such as Aldous Huxley, C.S. Lewis, Lord

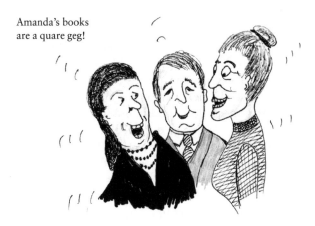

Amanda's books
are a quare geg!

Oxford, Sir Edward Grey and so on, who competed amongst themselves to see who could read her work aloud for the longest period of time without laughing. She received correspondence from many famous people because they enjoyed her replies. She wrote two books of poetry, *Fumes of Formation* and *Poems of Puncture*, and fumed when Barry Paine gave her books bad reviews. She said his work would disappear while hers would last a thousand years. The irony is that if the critic hadn't damned her writing, both of them would have been long forgotten.

When Amanda visited Westminster Abbey, she wrote:

Holy Moses! Have a look!
Flesh decayed in every nook!
Some rare bits of brawn are here
Mortal lumps of beef and beer,
Some of them are turned to dust,
Everyone bids lost to lust;
Royal flesh so tinged with 'blue'
Undergoes the same as you.
Famous some were – yet they died;
Poets – Statesmen – Rogues beside,
Kings – Queens, all of them do rot,
What about them? Now – they're not!

Amanda thought that it was unfair for everyone to eventually return to dust. She believed people of superior breeding and talent, such as herself, should return to pebbles!

Andy Ross died in August 1917, after thirty years of marriage. He'd just finished a meal she'd cooked and as a memento she preserved a pea pod from one of the peas of his last meal. She was pleased he departed this earth on a full stomach but she was very upset. She wanted to be left alone with what she referred to as her 'great grief' but Andy had been very popular. People wanted to pay their respects and sent wreaths – Amanda hired a boy with a wheelbarrow to return them to people she didn't like. She told the undertakers the moment Andy's body was placed inside the hearse to make the horses break into a trot. As a result, mourners, complete with top hats and frock coats, who had come to walk in a funeral cortege, had to either run after the coffin or return home, which most of them did!

Amanda stopped writing after Andy died. Eventually she met and married a wealthy farmer, who lived near Ballynahinch. She mellowed with age and retired, living quietly and contentedly in County Down. She was a strange mixture. She could be kind and thoughtful yet when roused exhibited a vicious, vindictive and foul temper. She died believing she was a great authoress without realising her novels are in fact so awful they are hilariously funny. During the whole of her long life she didn't realise she was a source of great amusement. She remained confident she was a literary giant and even thought of applying for a Nobel Prize in English Literature.

CAPTAIN THOMAS MAYNE REID, AUTHOR

Captain Thomas Mayne Reid (1818–1883) was born at Ballyroney Manse, near Banbridge. His family wanted him to be a clergyman. They must have been disappointed when he went to America and served in the US Army during the Mexican War. After he left America he lived in London and wrote thrilling adventure tales for boys. He is buried in Kensal Green Cemetery, London.

HARRY FERGUSON, ENGINEER AND INVENTOR

Harry Ferguson (1884–1960) was born in Lake House, Magheraconluce Road, near Dromore, the fourth of Mary and James Ferguson's eleven children. He was an unhappy child because his farmer parents were strict fundamentalists. He hated farming and became an agnostic in spite of, or perhaps because of, his family's best efforts. Local people say he was a wild child, who was expelled from Ballykeel National School. He finished his full-time education at the age of 15 and worked around the family farm.

Harry was constantly at loggerheads with his father and planned to escape by emigrating to Canada, but his brother Joe offered him an apprenticeship at his car workshop in Belfast. He loved to tinker with engines, quickly became a first-rate mechanic and helped to establish his brother's workshop as the best in Belfast. He took part in motorcycle races and used the events to publicise his brother's business. He won many races and built a reputation as a fearless and determined rider, nicknamed the 'Mad Mechanic'. As a result, his brother Joe's business, J.B. Ferguson & Co., received excellent publicity.

Harry became fascinated by flying. He visited air shows at Blackpool and Reims and convinced his brother that building and flying a plane would be good for business. He had numerous accidents and at one point had to use a stick as a walking aid. However, in 1909 he flew approximately 100 yards down the shore at Newcastle, becoming the first man in Ireland to fly a plane. He won £100, which was a considerable amount of money at the time, and he was the first person in the British Isles to both build and fly his own plane.

Harry began courting Maureen Watson, the daughter of a Dromore grocer. They got married in 1913. People living in

Dromore say they think she put her foot down and insisted he stopped doing dangerous things like flying!

In 1911 Harry left his brother Joe's business and opened his own firm, May Street Motors, in Belfast and kickstarted his inventing career. At that time there was a food shortage and the Irish Board of Agriculture asked Harry to improve the efficiency of tractors, which would speed up food production.

In 1928, after years of work, Harry patented his invention, the hydraulic three-point linkage Ferguson System. People around Dromore said the invention wasn't entirely Harry Ferguson's idea and that a local man, Willy Sands, had a lot to do with it. It revolutionised world farming, resulting in improved productivity and saving lives because older tractors had a tendency to upend and kill the driver. One of Harry's original black tractors now resides in the Science Museum in London.

Harry decided his invention should start earning some serious money by going into mass production so he went to America and met Henry Ford. Harry's demonstration of his newly developed tractor impressed Ford so much that the pair shook hands and entered into a gentlemen's agreement and before long Ford-Ferguson tractors were rolling off the production line. When Henry Ford died and his grandson refused to honour the gentlemen's agreement, Harry entered into a lengthy legal battle against the Ford Motor Company and won.

Yon tractor wot Harry Ferguson designed was some yoke.

Harry remained enthusiastic about winning a worldwide market for his tractor and approached Standard Motors; in 1946 they started mass producing the tractor that became known as the Little Grey Fergie.

He was an excellent salesman, who pulled off the PR coup of the decade by driving one of his little grey tractors through Claridge's Hotel in London. The little grey tractor is thought to be the world's most famous tractor. Over half a million were sold over the ten years it was in production.

Harry must have become bored with slow-moving tractors because he turned his attention to motor cars. He was instrumental in establishing the Ulster Grand Prix and Tourist Trophy Motor Cycle Races. He developed a four-wheel drive car and anti-skid braking. He remained very aware of the importance of publicity and demonstrated the value of his four-wheel drive system by installing it in a Formula 1 car. In 1961 his car, the P99, became the world's first, and only, Formula 1-winning four-wheel drive car when Stirling Moss drove it to victory. Unfortunately, Harry didn't live long enough to see Moss's victory or the popularity of four-wheel drive vehicles in the car industry. He was found dead, aged 75, in his bath at home in Stow-on-the Wold on 25 October 1960. He suffered from insomnia and depression and had taken an overdose of barbiturates. The coroner was unable to say whether his death was an accident or suicide.

It's possible to visit the homestead where Harry Ferguson was born, on the Magheraconluce Road, near Dromore. He's commemorated by a sculpture of an aeroplane on the left of the flyover bridge leading to Hillsborough on Northern Ireland's A1, going towards Belfast.

JOSEPH SCRIVEN, AUTHOR

Joseph Medlicott Scriven (1819–1886) was born in Ballymoney Lodge, near Banbridge. The house is marked by a blue plaque and can be seen on the left side of the A1 dual carriageway when travelling towards Belfast, having left Banbridge via the exit nearest Dromore. His old homestead looks like a white farmhouse. It's set well back from the road and is surrounded by trees.

Joseph Scriven's baptism was entered in the church records of Seapatrick Parish Church on 10 September 1819. His father, Captain John Scriven of the Royal Marines, was, on two occasions, a churchwarden of Seapatrick Parish Church. His mother, Jane Medlicott, was the sister of the Revd Joseph Medlicott, a vicar in Wiltshire. Joseph was their second child.

By 1845 Joseph had been awarded a degree from Trinity College, Dublin and was looking forward to his forthcoming marriage, intending to set up house locally. Unfortunately, the day before the young couple were due to be married his fiancée was crossing a bridge over the River Bann on horseback and her horse threw her. She hit her head, became unconscious and drowned in the river.

Joseph was heartbroken. He left the Anglican Church and joined the Plymouth Brethren, a very strict, fundamentalist Christian organisation. This caused strains within his family, which possibly resulted in him deciding to migrate to Canada. There he met, fell in love with and became engaged to Eliza Roche.

He shared the same religious beliefs as his fiancée. She had to be baptised in Rice Lake before they got married. It was early spring, the water was freezing cold, Eliza caught a chill which turned to pneumonia and she died. After that tragedy Joseph took a vow of poverty, sold all his worldly goods and spent the rest of his life giving practical help to people, such as cutting up firewood to keep the fires of the poor and needy burning. He became so poor he couldn't afford the fare home when his mother became seriously ill. He wanted to comfort her so he wrote a poem, *What a Friend We Have in Jesus*, and sent it to her:

What a Friend we have in Jesus, all our sins and griefs to bear!
What a privilege to carry everything to God in prayer!
O what peace we often forfeit, O what needless pain we bear,
All because we do not carry everything to God in prayer.

He never claimed authorship of his poem although he once said, 'The Lord and I wrote it together.'

Joseph Scriven's poem was discovered by chance by an American lawyer, Charles Converse. It was set to music and published as the hymn we know and love.

Some time after Joseph died his hymn came to the attention of a famous American Evangelist, Dwight L. Moody. He said that it was the most touching one he'd ever seen and brought it to a wider audience.

Unfortunately, Joseph Scriven came to a sad end. He was found drowned in Rice Lake on 10 August 1886. He was buried in Pengelley Cemetery next to Eliza Roche. His death was a great shock to a friend, who said:

'About midnight. I withdrew to an adjoining room, not to sleep, but to watch and wait. You may imagine my surprise and dismay when on visiting the room I found it empty. All search failed to find a trace of the missing man, until a little after noon the body was discovered in the water nearby, lifeless and cold in death.'

The big question is, did Joseph Scriven commit suicide? He was very depressed at the time, there's no doubt about that. However, his great nephew, the Rt Revd Henry Scriven, came to Holy Trinity Church in April 2002 and dedicated a stained-glass window to the memory of Joseph Scriven. A competition had been organised through local schools to design a memorial window. It was won by Louise McCann, a pupil of Newbridge Integrated School. I was present when the then rector, Archdeacon John Scott, asked the Rt Revd Henry Scriven if he thought Joseph had committed suicide? The Rt Revd Henry Scriven replied, 'I don't believe he did. He was such a strict, sincere Christian he'd have thought suicide was against God's Will and wouldn't have ended his God-given life. I am sure his death was accidental or perhaps the result of a massive stroke, or something. Accurate autopsies were not available at the time.'

There's a memorial garden in Downshire Place, Banbridge, dedicated to Joseph Scriven.

HOWARD FERGUSON, COMPOSER

Howard Ferguson (1908–1999) was a distinguished composer, commissioned by BBC NI to compose 'Overture for an Occasion' to celebrate Queen Elizabeth II's coronation in 1953. He was a member of Banbridge's Ferguson linen family.

F.E. MCWILLIAM, SCULPTOR

Frederick Edward McWilliam (1909–1992) was born in Newry Street, Banbridge, the son of a local doctor. He was educated locally and attended Belfast College of Art before enrolling in the Slade School of Fine Art in London, where he trained as a sculptor.

Mac, as he was known, said:

> I think I was lucky born where I was in a country town; Banbridge made most of the things it needed … and of course Banbridge was a linen town – the mill dams gave us swimming pools in summer, blue fields when the flax was in flower, and white fields when the linen was spread out to bleach. Magical intrusions in the normal patchwork of green.

His old home is now a shop. It is marked by a blue plaque.

Marjorie Burnett was a close friend of Mac. She called him 'Freddie' and they corresponded until his death on 13 May 1992. When I first met her Marjorie she was a great old lady and no local function was complete without her pancakes. She never married and was very upset when 'Freddie' died. She recalled:

> Freddie was like a brother to me. When I think about it, it's a wonder we weren't killed when we were youngsters! The slightest skiff of snow and the pair of us used to take tin trays up to the top of the Yellow Hill [the steep hill that leads out

of the town towards Newry. It was thought to be associated with fairies as denoted by the reference to the colour yellow] and slid all the way down to the bottom of the town. It was great fun! We never could understand why our fun made our parents so cross! Now I realise the danger of dodging in and out among horses' hooves. At the time we thought we were just risking a good hiding!

In 1932 Mac married Elizabeth Esther Rounds. The young couple rented a cottage in Chartridge, Buckinghamshire, which they shared with Henry Moore.

Mac's first sculptures were semi-abstract, then he visited the International Surrealist Exhibition in London (1936) and became influenced by what he saw. He never became fully surrealist. He said, 'What appealed to me in Surrealism was it made for freedom of thinking – I should put it this way, I was for Surrealism, but not with it.'

In 1939 Mac had his first one-man show at the London Gallery, Cork Street, London. He joined the RAF on the outbreak of war, serving in England and later in India. When he returned to London in 1946 he began to experiment in a wide range of media as well as teaching at the Chelsea School

Ah! Get away with ye, Willie John, ye don't say yer wheelman Freddie McWilliam from Banbridge became internationally famous!

of Art for a year before taking up a post at The Slade, which he held until 1968.

Mac became an internationally renowned sculptor, known and respected by other famous sculptors, including Elizabeth Frink, who was commissioned to produce a sculpture to decorate a bank in Shaftesbury Square, Belfast. (It consists of two abstract bodies, suspended one above the other on the bank's walls and is known locally as 'Draft and Overdraft'!)

In 1949 Mac and his family moved to a house and studio in Holland Park. When he died his estate gifted the contents of his studio and some sculptures to Banbridge District Council. After several years of research, a suitable site and funding were secured to open a purpose-built gallery, with a replica of F.E. McWilliam's studio and a sculpture garden. The gallery opened in 2008 and features a permanent display of Mac's work, temporary exhibitions of Irish and international art, a craft shop, visitor information point and an award-winning café. Admission is free, there's ample parking and it's well worth a visit.

Mac's daughter, Bridget, married the Welsh painter Augustus John's grandson.

HELEN WADDELL, AUTHOR

Helen Waddell (1889–1965) was born in Tokyo, the daughter of a Presbyterian minister. The family moved back to Belfast when she was 11. She became a bestselling author in 1933 when her only novel, *Peter Abelard*, was published. It was a love story firmly grounded in meticulous academic research. She had close connections with County Down and frequently stayed with her sister Meg at Kinmacrew House, Magherally. She is buried in the family grave in Magherally churchyard, near Banbridge.

6

COUNTY DOWN AND THE GREAT FAMINE

In general, Irish people, North and South, suffered terribly during the famine years. It was caused by failure of the potato crop. There were a few isolated spots that escaped; however, the overall population was decimated by starvation and disease and decreased from over 8½ million to 3½ million. People gleaned whatever food they could find from the wild.

Some memories have survived in the form of family oral history as grandparents reminisce about their ancestors attempting to catch fish, gathering nettles for soup and blackberries for tarts. As a result, foraging became socially unacceptable. It suggested poverty. With increasing prosperity, delicacies such as nettle soup, blackberry puddings and fish dishes have reappeared and are on the menus of upmarket restaurants.

Northern Ireland had the largest percentage of small farms in the whole of Ireland. That is farms of less than 5 acres. The farms had been sub-divided because families were large – fourteen children was not unusual. Parents wanted to enable their offspring to be independent so gave them a patch of land. The linen industry was thriving as a cottage industry and was used to subsidise incomes. Farmers either grew flax and sold the part of the plant that could be spun into linen threads or set up a loom at home and wove cloth (see Chapter 7).

Linen cloth is very strong and was used to make sails for ships during the Napoleonic Wars (1803–1815). After the war ended, and all necessary repairs to ships' sails had been done, the industry went into recession.

In the 1830s the use of linen was challenged by cotton and industrialisation. Spinning was mechanised, weaving began to be mechanised, and the wages of weavers dropped.

Life was harsh in the nineteenth century. There were public executions throughout the country. Gallows, used to hang people who had been classified as criminals, were a common sight and could be seen in such places as Church Square, Banbridge, Gallows Street in Dromore and outside Downpatrick Jail, now Downpatrick Museum. They were used well into the 1800s.

In 1832 there was an inquiry into poverty in England that resulted in the English Poor Law System being set up. It found there was greater poverty in Ireland than in England. For example, in Dromore the poor lived in houses that were always damp. They slept on straw on the floor or on beds made of sticks supported by stones with potatoes stored under them, and they piled heaps of manure beside the door. Manure was a precious commodity because it was used to fertilise crops. It was a tragedy if it was stolen. At that time the significance of disease-bearing organisms had not been discovered and as a result life expectancy was low.

William Makepeace Thackeray travelled throughout Ireland and said Newry was the only town he had seen that didn't have people living in 'huts' around its perimeter. These 'huts' were 'houses' built from sods of earth piled on top of each other and thatched with anything at hand, such as straw, gorse and so on. They soaked up damp in Ireland's wet climate and had a lifespan of approximately ten years.

During 'A commission to inquire into the Condition of the Poorer Classes in Ireland' (1833–34) statements were taken from the clergy regarding the living conditions of the poor. The clergy came from different places but their statements are similar. Regarding the poor in his parish, Dromore, Revd S.C. Nelson said:

There are 160 mere labourers. Of these, not more than 50 are in constant work: beside these, some holders of 5 acre farms labour occasionally for the larger farmers who plough their fields, or give them provision as payment ... They are least employed from December to April, and from the middle of May to the middle of July; the latter period is the most trying, potatoes being scarce and bad ... Women are occasionally employed in reaping and potato-gathering, at 6d per day, and the children in potato-gathering at 3d or 4d per day.

Regarding the ordinary diet and clothing of the poor, the Revd Nelson said:

In summer, potatoes and buttermilk thrice daily. In winter, potatoes with salt or onions or occasionally salt herring; infrequently oatmeal porridge; they scarcely ever taste flesh-meat; their clothing universally ragged and uncomfortable.

He told the inquiry that the yearly expense for an able-bodied labourer in full work would be:

Potatoes and milk thrice daily would cost him about £6; potatoes and milk for breakfast and supper in summer, oatmeal porridge in winter, potatoes and butter also occasionally flesh meat, would cost, during any of the last three years, about £8 or £9.

The Revd Nelson described the living conditions of the poor as follows:

The dwellings are of stones and road mortar, or mud walls, or sods; a close window of one or two panes; floors always damp from under water and want of air. In town their bed is straw, on the floor, with a blanket, and sometimes a quilt; in country, the same, with a bedstead of rude sticks supported on stones, beneath which is kept a store of potatoes; they are very wretched ... since the peace of 1815 conditions have greatly deteriorated, chiefly owing to a decline in the linen trade.

The Revd James Davis, a Non-Subscribing Presbyterian minister representing Seapatrick and Banbridge, told the inquiry:

> The wants of the poorest households in this neighbourhood appear to me to be chiefly the following :- the want of fuel, the want of bedding, the want of clothing and the want of dry lodgings. Bad fires, bad food, cold damp houses and bad clothing.

The 1833–1834 investigation into the living conditions of the poor resulted in Ireland being given its own poor law in August 1838 and workhouses were built to help the starving poor. County Down had four workhouses: Downpatrick, Newry, Newtownards and Banbridge.

To save expense the majority of workhouses were built to a plan drawn by George Wilkinson, who was employed by the Irish Poor Law Commissioners. The best-preserved workhouse in Northern Ireland is in Armagh. It's now part of St Luke's Hospital. The old workhouses had impressive exteriors but the interiors were finished as cheaply as possible. They were without ceilings and so on.

Banbridge Workhouse was similar to the one in Armagh and, like many other workhouses, was universally hated. It was eventually demolished and a hospital was built on part of the site. It too has since been demolished and the site now contains Banbridge Medical Centre, a polyclinic, housing for local doctors' medical practices, and an old people's home built on the site of the old fever hospital and a famine garden, with a very attractive sculpture. Unfortunately, only one of the workhouse minute books survived and a page of the book, recording the names of some of the inmates, was used in the sculpture. Bodies in unmarked graves were discovered when the new medical centre was being built. They, unlike many famine victims, had been decently buried in wooden coffins. They were reinterred in the cemetery on the Newry Road.

Banbridge Workhouse was built in 1841 at a cost of £10,000 to hold 800 residents. It served an area stretching from

The peasants are disgusting. Their clothes are dirty and torn. They must have done something awful and God is punishing them.

Tandragee in the east, Leitrim in the west, Dromore in the north and Glaskermore in the south. In the early 1840s it rarely held more than 300 people but things changed during the Great Famine, when one-third of the area's population were dependent on potatoes, and they came flooding in.

In January 1847 the workhouse was full and admissions had to be halted. Whooping cough caused fifty-four people to be turned away. Flu and dysentery were prevalent. The staff found it impossible to cope so the guardians began negotiations to rent the brewery as additional accommodation. They erected sheds and added galleries wherever possible. It is important to remember that all this happened in Banbridge, one of the most prosperous places in Ulster.

The temporary fever hospital, at the back of the workhouse, became overcrowded. Smallpox spread throughout Banbridge and there were three cases of cholera in Dromore. For three weeks in a row the master, Mr Sheridan, had to turn away more than 300 applicants for admission to the workhouse and on 13 March 1847 he had to call police to disperse starving people demanding admission.

On 8 February 1848 the workhouse had 1,464 inmates. After that there was a slow decline in numbers but they never fell below 1,000 until the summer of 1848.

Workhouses were terrible places. The process of entering one was designed to be humiliating. The staff stripped you naked, shoved you in a bath, cut off your hair, scrubbed you with harsh carbolic soap, dressed you in ugly, ill-fitting workhouse clothes and provided a pair of shoes that probably didn't fit and caused blisters.

The workhouse system was very cruel. Families were divided, with men in one section, women in another. Children never saw their parents and brothers were separated from sisters. This applied to children as young as 2 years of age. Inmates had to work hard, scrubbing floors, spinning, weaving, milling corn, sewing rough sack cloth, splitting rocks and picking oakum (oakum was rope covered in tar. The tar had to be picked off the rope and the threads separated. It was dirty, unpleasant work that was hard on the hands). Even women were expected to split rocks, and any unsatisfactory work resulted in being thrown out of the workhouse to starve.

There was no privacy. Inmates slept together on wooden platforms in wards. Each ward contained two large tubs to act as toilets and the smell was revolting.

In those days no job meant no income. The workhouse was the alternative to starving and it was means tested. Help was not available to anyone owning more than a quarter acre of land.

In December 1846 the Lord Lieutenant of Ireland demanded a meeting of ratepayers in Castlewellan so they could agree to pay into a fund for public works for famine relief. Arthur Wills Blundell Sandys Trumbull Hill, the 3rd Marquess of Downshire and Banbridge's landlord, was annoyed. He wrote a letter to his tenants and ratepayers on his Upper Iveagh Estate saying they should go to the meeting to protect their interests. He felt their rights 'may be voted away by any rabble that choose to assemble, with the object of overawing and bullying holders, who alone are entitled to vote'. They could end up paying 'for the purpose of carrying on useless or injurious works as has been so frequently the case in the South and West of Ireland'.

His Lordship had a point. The relief schemes were badly organised. Wages were often not paid for long periods because of bureaucracy. Men were literally starved to death on public works schemes, building useless roads that stopped halfway up boggy hillsides, with a small bowl of rice as payment. Over 400,000 people were supposed to be employed through them and landlords felt the pinch because rents were not paid.

Lord Trevelyn, Assistant Secretary to the British Treasury, ordered that landlords should not profit from the schemes. He believed in market forces and refused to do anything that would interfere with them. As a result, rents went up and wages went down, and the price of grain was set above its market value. Agricultural improvements and growing alternative crops were forbidden. In other words, landlords were not allowed to do anything useful! Wages were low to avoid undercutting the labour market, despite the fact that ordinary labour was almost extinct. The death rate soared while the government insisted the Irish were exaggerating their plight; coffins became in short supply so paupers were buried in pits.

The Public Works Scheme was so unsatisfactory that it was discontinued and soup kitchens were introduced. They kept people alive. In the spring of 1847, during one day, 4,000 people queued for soup in Loughbrickland.

Many people emigrated both before and after the famine. That necessitated a hazardous journey. James Rintoul of Dufferin Cottage wrote to his brother in 1857, saying, 'It took three months for our ship to arrive in Toronto ... nearly every day corpses were put overboard and public worship was held on deck.' It's been said that if a cross had been erected for very immigrant who died at sea the Atlantic Ocean would resemble a closely packed graveyard.

Emigrant ships were stopped at a quarantine station, on Grosse Isle, Canada. Many passengers had cholera or typhus. The immigrants landed and were counted before being housed in small tents. Boilers were supplied and they were forced to boil their clothes before proceeding further. If the weather was bad, boiling their few clothes resulted in a few miserable nights while they dried. People suffering from typhus or cholera were housed in separate tents and their families were not allowed to visit them. Many immigrants were buried on the island.

7

THE LINEN INDUSTRY

It's possible to visit the last linen-producing factory in Ireland, Ferguson's Mills in Banbridge.

Linen threads are formed inside flax plants as tubes, called phloem, used to pass food around inside the plant. Flax plants have unusually strong phloem, enabling them to be processed to form a hardwearing cloth.

Until the early part of the eighteenth century most farmers produced a little flax, which they dressed and wove into linen for their own use. They sold any leftover yarn.

During the last 300 years flax growing has been linked to large-scale commercial production of linen. More flax was grown in Ulster than in any of Ireland's Provinces and the Bann Valley was the centre of the linen industry.

Flax is a greedy plant, taking a lot of moisture out of the soil. To ensure a good crop, it was usually grown in a plant succession on ground that had been heavily manured for potatoes. Little flax is grown today. It is imported, mostly from Belgium.

The ground was usually ploughed two or three times and flax seed was sown broadcast. Sowing in drills resulted in a wide space between plants and the growth of short side stems of little value.

Well ploughed land is relatively weed free, but the crop was weeded during the eighteenth and nineteenth centuries by women and children crawling on their hands and knees. It was flattened as they crawled over it but the plants recovered

I'm broadcasting flax seed. What do you think I'm doing, frying eggs?

quickly, provided they were less than 14cm (approximately 6in when pulled out by the roots) in length.

Great expertise was needed to decide when to harvest the flax – too soon and the fibres were soft and weak, too late and they were too thick to make the finest linen.

The phloem fibres in flax extend into the roots, so it was harvested by being pulled out, by the roots, by hand, until the 1940s. They were pulled upwards and slightly to one side. Four handfuls of flax made one beet (sheaf), which was tied with a piece of rush plant because, unlike string and rope, rushes do not rot in water.

Once the flax was pulled, immature seeds were removed by being pulled with a structure called a 'rippling comb' formed by a plank that had a set of 25cm (10in) iron teeth driven into it. The rippling comb was often placed into the back of a cart so the seeds could be collected. They were used to feed animals or make linseed oil. It wasn't possible to produce good linen and seeds because by the time the seeds had formed the phloem fibres were too thick.

We are rippling the flax plants to remove the seeds.

When the beets had been rippled, around the middle of August, they were placed into a flax dam, also called a lint hole, to rot (retted).

Lint dams were narrow holes designed so the workers could 'fork' the beets from each side, using an agricultural fork. The beets were weighed down by large stones. Those destined to make fine linen were placed at the bottom of the dam, with coarse beets at the top because they retted comparatively quickly and could be removed first.

The time the beets were kept in the dam depended on the weather, the quality of the water and the type of flax. Farmers became expert at knowing when the beets were ready for if they got it wrong they risked losing the entire crop.

It took about two weeks for the plant material around the phloem to rot, after which scantily dressed men jumped into the lint dam and threw the beets out onto the side. It was dirty, smelly work. The whole countryside reeked when a lint dam was opened.

The late Dr Bill Crawford told me that when he was a boy he loved to work in a lint dam because he was able to wear his old clothes and get covered in filthy slime without getting into trouble. Only young boys and old men, without any interest in women, would get into a lint dam! The smell, like that of a skunk, could persist for several weeks.

Once out of the dam the beets needed to be dried. Some farmers used a method similar to haymaking. They waited until the flax was almost dry, then 'gaited' it by picking up large handfuls so that the roots were all together, tied it near the top and spread the bottom of the plant stems out to form a wide base on which the gaitin stood. Gaitins were left standing in the field for a few days then built into a rick. During this time the field could not be put to other uses.

My old friend, the late Ernest Scott, described another, more economical method of drying gaitins. He said: 'Cut branches out of hedges, stick them into the ground, tie twine between the branches to form a type of fence and tie the gaitins up to dry on the twine. Within a few hours gaitins dried by this method were

I'm not getting into any flax dam nohow! It would make me stink for days and the weemen wouldn't fancy me!

ready to be formed into ricks and the field was free for other use.'

Once it was dry the flax was taken to be scutched, which was usually done in a scutch mill. According to Ernest, you had to wait your turn to go to the scutch mill. There was an old saying, 'Short accounts mean long friends.' In other words, if the scutch mill's account was settled promptly, waiting was reduced the following year. Scutching was a dangerous process in which unwanted dried parts of the plant were knocked off the linen fibres. The flax was 'bruised' by being run through wooden rollers to make stiff, dried plants pliable and loosen and remove unwanted plant parts. Then the flax was taken over to a wooden post, or 'stock', and hit with a blunt wooden blade. This knocked the unwanted parts of the plant off, leaving the phloem fibres, which formed linen threads. The fibres were hackled by being put through a 'hackling comb' to make sure they were all lying the same way. Spinning turns short fibres into a long yarn.

Before industrialisation women worked at home with spinning wheels. The spun threads were wound into 'hanks' that were boiled before being turned into cloth.

Scutching was dangerous because it was dark inside a scutch mill. A second's loss of concentration could result in mutilation or even death.

The *Down Recorder* on Saturday, 18 November 1893 reported the death of Annie Mulligan, an elderly crippled woman who worked in David McMordie's scutch mill at Drumaughis, near Crossgar. She was taking her place when she fell. Her hands landed on teethed rollers and were pulled off. Before help could arrive, her scalp had been pulled off and her body was mangled.

Scutch mills' air became clouded with highly flammable dust, so they frequently burnt down. The dust got into workers' lungs and aggravated any tendency to suffer lung disease.

The waste left over from scutching was called 'chowes'. It was collected by the poor and used for stuffing things such as mattresses.

Wages were very low. Men worked at the loom for fourteen hours a day for a net income of 4 shillings a day, or less.

Many families existed on a sort of gruel made of the cheapest sort of Indian meal eaten twice a day, others lived on boiled cabbage with a little oatmeal sprinkled over it. The linen merchants grew rich and built mansions.

Barbour Threads, the biggest producer of threads in the world, had a huge mill in Gilford. It started off belonging to Dunbar McMaster before being taken over by the Barbour family, who also owned Hilden Mill and a mill in America.

According to Nora Bates, the nature of the work meant windows couldn't be opened. She was born in Saintfield and described working during the 1940s in the mill in Comber, owned by John Andrews. She said the air was dry and full of dust and sometimes she was sent to work in one of the rooms where she had to stand, barefoot, in water all day.

Nora was a 'spreader' when she started work in the mill. The flax threads came along on a conveyer belt. She made sure they were straight before they disappeared into a tunnel at the end of the room.

Once the threads had been spun they were loaded onto huge bobbins and woven into cloth. The work was dangerous because bobbins and shuttlecocks could fly unexpectedly around the room, causing serious injury. Cowdy's Mill, in Banbridge, had such a terrible reputation for death and injury during the 1950s that it was referred to as Belsen. Nobody ever got any

Linen from the loom's brown so I'm spreading it out in the sun to bleach and turn white.

compensation because the owners argued the worker had been in the wrong place at the time.

Linen straight from the loom was a dark brown colour. It was bleached, by the sun, to turn it white by being spread out on bleaching greens. Seeing fields covered in linen was once a common sight. Linen is a valuable crop so watchtowers were built and men hired to shelter inside to keep the linen from being stolen or damaged by straying cows. A watchtower once situated at Tullylish has been rebuilt in the Ulster Folk and Transport Museum.

Penalties for stealing linen were severe. Starving people, who'd stolen linen to buy food, could have had a hand cut off, be transported, or hung.

According to the *Belfast Newsletter* of 11 April 1783, the following people were found guilty of stealing linen and received the following sentences:

Patrick Gordon to be executed at Drumbridge on Thursday next the 17th inst. and Stephen Gordon to be executed at Castlewellan on Monday next inst. for stealing linen out of the bleach green.

While storytelling in Sumter, South Carolina, in 1992, I met a charming African-American gentleman who had the same surname as me. He said, 'The oral history of my family states my McBride ancestor received what I now understand to be a light sentence for stealing linen. He was transported and sold as a slave in Jamaica and eventually ended up in South Carolina.'

The gentleman's features had a startling resemblance to those of my husband! It's one of the great regrets of my life that I didn't get his address. I tried to trace him when I returned home and was surprised to hear there's a colony of black McBrides in Sumter.

The Bann Valley was the main centre of the linen industry. Today it's lined with the remains of linen mills and associated mansions, two of which have been turned into hotels, the Belmont and the Banville. It's worth the price of a cup of coffee to nose round an interesting old building and catch a glimpse into how people once lived there.

The Belmont Hotel was built in 1838 for Robert McClellan, who owned the Bann Weaving Factory. It's been described by Charles Brett as 'an excellent example of the Greek Revival style at its best'.

The next owner was William Anderson, nicknamed 'Jumbo' because he was a big man, standing at over 6ft in height and weighing 20 stone. He was a keen sportsman who hunted and took part in hare coursing with his greyhound, Sir Sankey. He was a member of the Royal Ulster Yacht Club, Bangor and owned a yacht, the *Satanella*, which he had anchored there. He used to sail to America, Canada, the Mediterranean and the Middle East. He brought back all sorts of souvenirs, carpets and rugs, most of which ended up in the Belmont.

He met his wife, Katherine Elizabeth Ida McNeill, when he was on a cruise around the Scottish Islands. They married in

1901 and had four children, three girls and a boy, William Brice, who was born on 9 February 1913. A Monkey Puzzle tree was planted at the side of the driveway to commemorate his birth.

Brice recalled that his mother was always late and when she travelled to Belfast she used to phone the station and ask them to hold the train until she arrived. They invariably agreed!

One day she decided to travel to Belfast by car. Cairns, the chauffeur, had never been there before and ended up driving behind a tram. Katherine became impatient and ordered, 'For goodness sake, hurry up and pass that tram.' Cairns replied, 'Is that what it is? I've been waiting for it to move over.'

King Edward VII's coronation was delayed because he nearly died from appendicitis, so removing children's appendixes was thought advisable. Jumbo bought an operating table, set it up in the dining room and hired a surgeon to remove his children's appendixes. Brice remembered being told to stay in bed one day. A surgeon came into his room and knocked him out with chloroform. When he woke up he had a huge scar in his side, complete with ten large stitches. In later life he delighted in showing his scar to family, friends and acquaintances!

Jumbo died, aged 66, on 14 May 1927 and was buried in Banbridge Municipal Cemetery. The house and contents were sold to the Finney family.

8

COUNTY DOWN DURING THE WORLD WARS

THE SINKING OF THE KILKEEL FISHING FLEET

Kilkeel fishing fleet was sunk by a German U-boat on Ascension Thursday, 30 May 1918. Tommy Doonan's boat, *Never Can Tell*, was one of the boats sunk. He left an account of what happened.

The *Never Can Tell* had put into Clogher Head, a small port just south of Dundalk in the Republic of Ireland. Tommy recalled seeing the women in their finery and the men dressed in their best suits heading for church and hearing the church bells ring as they slipped anchor and sailed away.

When they got out to sea they saw the Kilkeel fishing fleet and sailed towards it. As they drew close to the fleet they shot their nets. Tommy said:

> We sighted a submarine surfacing a little distance off our starboard beam. He didn't appear interested in us and what we were doing. But as we rounded to come on to our nets he fired six shots across our bows. We knew then that he meant business. It was a U-boat. It came along the *Never Can Tell* and that was when I saw the machine gun. Just you picture it – us standing on our wee boat, looking down the barrel and not knowing if, or when, it would start firing. The U-boat Commander shouted 'Have you any guns?' and like one man we shouted, 'No!'

The U-boat Commander shouted, 'I want to speak to your skipper.' Paddy Kearney yelled back, 'I'm in charge.' The German shouted, 'We're coming aboard.' One of his sailors jumped onto the deck of the *Never Can Tell*, clutching either a bomb or a grenade, Tommy couldn't be sure which. Whatever it was, the German knocked it sharply on the rail of the fishing boat, flung it into the hold and demanded the crew board the submarine. Tommy said:

When we were all aboard – and it didn't take long I can tell you because there was plenty of encouragement in the hold – we were mustered, with hands above our heads, along the conning tower casing. The engines came alive, and we moved a little to starboard. The U-boat pulled away and headed in the direction of the *Saint Mary*, another Kilkeel boat fishing some distance away. Behind us, deserted and lonely looking, we left our wee ship drifting, but not for long. There was a muffled 'thump', her mast fell and she slid back down into the water. It was all over very quickly. A sad sight for all of us. Heaving-to beside the *Saint Mary*, the German repeated the process, but this time he ordered the crew to take to their punt before blowing up their boat.

The U-boat sank the entire fleet: *Cyprus*, *Sparkling Wave*, *Honey Bee*, *Lloyds*, *Jane Gordo'n* and *Marianne McCrum* of Annalong. Then the U-boat turned north and sank three boats from the Ardglass fishing fleet. Tommy said:

With every sinking our spirits went down. Eventually the *Moss Rose* was the only fishing boat left. It was left all alone surrounded by the debris of the sunken ships and the small punts. We thought the *Moss Rose* was 'for it' too but when we came close to her the Germans put us aboard and told us 'When you get back to port tell your friends how badly the Germans treated you. I don't understand why good fishermen like you are not in the war.'

After the U-boat left the small boats kept close to the *Moss Rose*. Tommy's brother, James, met them in his boat the *Queen Bee* and towed the pathetic little school of small boats back to Kilkeel.

It appears that the U-boat commander went out of his way to ensure the safety of the fishermen. Why? U-boat commanders were not noted for humanitarianism! The commander had sunk the fishing fleet close to the shore in an area where the Royal Navy was active. It was wartime and he could have been forgiven if he hadn't worried about loss of life. The Germans asked some of the fishermen if they knew Mrs Collins of Mountain Road, Kilkeel. It transpired the Germans had been members of a German band that had toured the area before the war. They received the hospitality and friendliness for which the people of Mourne are famous. Perhaps that's why the fishermen's lives were spared.

THE AMERICANS

President Roosevelt is on record as having said, 'The Second World War could not have been won without the North of Ireland's War effort.' County Down played an active part by housing Americans involved in the war efforts, providing locations for them to practise skills necessary in war, looking after prisoners-of-war, repairing planes, growing linen and producing food. In addition, many people living in County Down joined the armed forces, although Northern Ireland did not have any conscription. Joining the armed forces was voluntary.

Mrs Francie Shaw (1900–1994) was a lovely, jolly lady who laughed heartily as she recalled the American troops stationed in Banbridge during the Second World war. She said:

> The Americans were a very friendly bunch who used to chal-lenge the locals in boxing matches. Wee Johnny McCourt was a game wee cock although he was no bigger than a

sparrow's fart. He fancied himself as a boxer, so he did, and he took up the challenge. He climbed up into the ring and began prancing around in great style, punching the air with his wee boxing gloves and doing all sorts of fancy footwork. Then the American champion climbed into the ring. He was a positive Goliath! Huge! Wee Johnny goggled in horror, then had bad bowel problems and all this stuff ran down his wee legs. A voice from the back yelled, 'Yer man's lost his gum shield!'

GERMAN PRISONERS OF WAR

When holidaying in a boat on Loch Erne we met an unlikely link with County Down in the form of a German lady, Miss Gros. She'd been a teacher in my husband's old school, Grosvenor High School, Belfast. He'd always liked her so we invited her back to our boat for a coffee. She was very interested to hear he was the Principal of Gilford Primary School. She said, 'I love Gilford. During the war I was placed there in a prisoner of war camp because I was a German national.'

We knew the government had rounded up all German nationals at the beginning of the Second World War but hadn't realised that perfectly innocent, good people like Miss Gros had been incarcerated. We said we didn't think that was fair and, to our surprise, she said:

Germans, who'd been working locally, were locked up in Gilford when the Second World War was declared. They had a great time!

It was wonderful! The people in Gilford were so good to us. They supplemented our rations by giving us treats. We'd good craic, enough work to keep us from being bored. Our guards locked us up at night and went home. We waited until the coast was clear then we got out under the wire at the back of the camp. We visited friends, or went and had craic in the local pubs. The locals, including our guards, welcomed us. We had a ball! I cried my eyes out when I was repatriated at the end of the war. We all did! We loved Ireland. The first thing we did on arriving in Germany was turn round and come straight back! I'm very happy here. I love the Irish and the way they have a way of getting round the law while appearing to obey it!

MILES AIRCRAFT

In 1942 Miles Aircraft Ltd received a request to produce an plane that could act as an observation and liaison aircraft. The plane, the Miles Messenger Mk II, was developed in three months. It first flew on 12 September 1942 and quickly became a technological success, with production moving to Walker's old linen factory in Banbridge. In its heyday it employed 200 people from the district. One of its employees, Tommy McMaster, said, 'Conditions in the old factory were far from ideal because it had lots of supporting columns and sometimes it was a bit of a puzzle juggling the long aircraft fuselages through the building.'

PETROL RATIONING

During the Second World War petrol was rationed in Northern Ireland. A friend, who doesn't want to be named, told me a story about wartime shenanigans. She says, 'A cousin learnt how to distil alcohol during a chemistry lesson at school and put his newfound knowledge to good use when he came home.'

The cousin, in cahoots with other relatives, set up a still in the large back garden of their house in a local town. It was well away from the property, out of sight of the law and beside a river, where evidence of their actions could be dumped if need be. Farmers were given petrol to use around the farm which was contaminated by a red dye to prevent it from being used in cars. The police checked petrol tanks regularly to make sure the vehicle was being run on legal fuel. The cousin's still was used to remove the red dye. The house became like a shebeen with people constantly coming and going, so the law became suspicious and a policeman called. An uncle invited him to search the house and yard, which gave those operating the still time to dismantle and hide it. After that the family decided to move operations to another family member's farm. It was up a long lane on top of a high hill. It was possible to access it over the fields. Everybody bought their legal quota of petrol and diluted it with the stuff they had distilled!

My father, Bill Henry, was very amused when, after the war, he met a retired customs officer who told him how he'd been puzzled by a lorry driver. The customs officer knew something illegal was happening but couldn't fathom what. Every day the lorry driver travelled over the border with an empty lorry and returned sometime later, again with an empty lorry. He was frequently stopped and searched but nothing was ever found. After he'd retired the customs officer met the lorry driver in a pub. He went over and said, 'It's too late for repercussions so please tell me what you were up to during the war. I know you were doing something illegal but can't figure what.'

The lorry driver laughed and said, 'That's easy! I made a fortune smuggling petrol. My lorry had a big petrol tank. I filled it, came home, sold the petrol and headed back down over the border with just enough juice to keep me going, filled my tank, headed home again and sold the petrol.'

D-DAY

Troops practised D-Day landings across the River Bann.

9

GHOSTS OF COUNTY DOWN

There are a lot of ghost stories and mysteries associated with County Down – too many to recount – so I've chosen a few I found particularly interesting.

THE FRIENDLY GHOSTS OF BALLYDUGAN FLOUR MILL

When Noel Killen was a wee lad riding his bicycle on the way to school he passed derelict Ballydugan Flour Mill, near Downpatrick, and dreamt about restoring it.

His dream came true. By dint of hard work he has recaptured the old mill's former glory and turned it into an award-winning venue for weddings. He says he loves being on a site that dates back to the sixteenth century and he's developed an interesting display about the mill's history on the fifth floor.

Folklore says that spirits have a tendency to return to places where they were happy in life and sometimes manifest themselves as ghosts. There are three happy ghosts in Ballydugan. I personally don't blame them for coming back because Noel has managed to retain the old mill's character while incorporating modern comforts.

Ballydugan's friendly ghosts attend weddings and bring luck. There's a Presbyterian minister who loiters around the basement and sometimes appears on the ground floor in the corner near the fire on the opposite side to the window.

'Yon ghost scared us! Mary said it would bring luck. It did! She had a big win on the lottery!'

Bobby danders around the first floor. He can be unpredictable. He usually appears as a silent shadow but sometimes he walks around slamming doors or he may be felt as a benign presence. And then there's a young girl, who is dressed in rough brown sackcloth. She loves to dance and may be seen dancing to the music provided at the wedding breakfast.

LORD BANGOR'S CAR

About twenty-five years ago I was telling ghost stories to a clatter of school children in the Ulster Folk and Transport Museum at Cultra when their teacher said, 'I think we've all seen ghosts and haven't realised it. I want to tell you a story.'

During the twenties and early thirties my father was a reporter for a local newspaper. He was sent to Castle Ward to write about their local fête. He hated doing that because it was so predictable. The same people won the same prizes every year. I can't remember their names but, to give you the idea I'll make names up, Big Aggie always won the prize for the best sponge, Bellowing Bertha took the soda bread prize, while Wee Will got the one for the best gladioli. Get the idea?

Well, on the day of the fête Dad caught the ferry from Portaferry early in the morning, crossed over to Strangford and began walking towards Castle Ward. He passed Annie, who lived in what was the last house in the village at the time. She was brushing the step around her front door and he stopped to have a bit of craic with her. When he continued his walk he saw a very old car driving along the road. It passed him. He reckoned it must have been built about 1904. It was dark green and it had a driver and three passengers. He waved at them. They didn't respond so he thought they were stuck up, the type of people who have lace curtains on the window and no sheets on the bed.

The fête was as boring as usual. The same people won the same prizes. It was a dead loss as far as writing anything interesting was concerned, then he remembered seeing the old car and thought, 'There could be a good story there.' He stopped at Annie's house and asked if she knew anything about the old car that had passed earlier in the morning. Annie said, 'I didn't see any cars this morning.' He said, 'You must have! It drove past me shortly after I was talking to you!'

Annie asked him to describe the car and said, 'You must have seen Lord Bangor's car. He and his friends were killed in a car accident years ago. The road has been re-routed since them days. The car didn't pass me. It would have gone through the hedge where the road used to be.'

MAGGIE'S LEAP

Deegan was a poacher, who had a beautiful daughter called Maggie. She was the apple of his eye and he taught her his poaching skills, which he used to provide food for the poor.

When Deegan became old and weak Maggie took over his work and became a poacher. She was an attractive girl with an hourglass figure and long flowing hair.

One day Maggie was walking to the south of Newcastle carrying a basket of poached birds' eggs when she was spotted by a group of soldiers. They started to chase her. She was frightened, ran away and became trapped in front of a deep chasm between the cliffs near Newcastle. She was terrified and decided she'd rather drown in the sea below, or be smashed on the rocks, than be caught by the soldiers. She took a deep breath, ran towards the chasm, leapt into the air and landed safely on the other side. Not an egg in her basket was broken.

Maggie lived to a ripe old age and eventually died of natural causes – her ghost is said to loiter around the place known as Maggie's Leap.

THE HELLFIRE CLUB IN COUNTY DOWN

Hellfire Club was the name for several exclusive clubs for high-society rakes established in Britain and Ireland in the eighteenth century. Legends of Black Masses and Satan worship have become attached to the club and members appear to have lived in County Down right up until the 1930s.

There are many colourful stories about Hellfire Clubs, including one about members of a club, who were drinking 'saltheen' (hot whiskey and melted butter) while standing in front of a roaring fire. The marrow in their bones melted so they dropped to the floor!

Members of a Hellfire Club always left an empty chair for the Devil and their mascot was a ferocious black cat. Folklore records that a brave clergyman went to one of their meetings and asked why the cat was served first. He was told because that it was the oldest person in the room. The cleric was terrified, panicked and said, 'That's not a cat! It's the Devil incarnate!' The club members were so annoyed they decided to kill the cleric.

He asked for a few moments to pray before being murdered. During his prayers he exorcised the cat. It changed into the Devil and shot up the chimney!

SQUIRE HAWKINS, LORD IVEAGH AND THE DEVIL

Squire Hawkins was an alderman to King Charles II. He fed and clothed the king's army. He did a good job and as a for reward his work the king gave him lands around Rathfriland that had been taken off Lord Iveagh, the Head of the Magennis Clan. Part of the old castle can still be seen today. It's said to be haunted by Lord Iveagh, who was so upset by the loss of his lands that he died and his ghost may be seen walking up and down, with its hands thrust deep inside his pockets. He looks as if he's trying to hold on to the remnants of his land and fortune.

The Hellfire Club, also known as the Order of the Friars of St Francis of Wycombe, began in the eighteenth century as an exclusive club for high-society libertines. It spread throughout England and Ireland. Squire Hawkins was a member when he lived in England and he became a founder member of Rathfriland's Hellfire Club.

Squire Hawkins was a cruel vindictive landlord, who was feared by the clean-living, God-fearing people in Rathfriland. He and his Hellfire shenanigans were hated by the local population and he literally gave his wife hell. She was a gentle woman and a staunch Christian, who attended Drumballyroney Church.

Eventually Squire Hawkins became terminally ill and died. During his illness he repeatedly said he was a Devil worshipper and he didn't want a Christian funeral.

After his death his wife did what most good wives do. She completely ignored her husband's wishes and arranged an elaborate funeral, with a team of eight fine horses to pull his hearse to Drumballyroney churchyard. The body was so reluctant to go it took the poor animals fifteen hours to reach their destination. When they reached the church gates the sky

I'm telling ye, when the rector looked out of the window the Devil himself was looking out of Squire Hawkins' grave.

darkened and the horses reared up. They refused to enter the churchyard and the coffin had to be lifted off the hearse and carried over to the grave, where it was committed to earth.

The next Sunday, when the rector was delivering his sermon, black clouds thundered above the church. There was a loud crash as a bolt of lightning flashed and struck the flat rock slab covering Squire Hawkins' grave. The rector glanced out the window and turned white with fear. The Devil was looking out of the grave.

After the service members of the congregation went and inspected the grave. The tombstone had been split to form the sign of the cross. Today it's difficult to make out the squire's name on the old tombstone, but the mark of the cross is clearly visible. As for Squire Hawkins himself – his ghost haunts the graveyard and the locals say God had his revenge on an evil man.

THE *LORD BLANEY*, GHOST SHIP AND HARBINGER OF DOOM

The *Lord Blaney*, a paddle steamer, foundered on the rocks near Prestatyn in Wales on 18 December 1833, while en route from Warrenpoint to Liverpool. Everyone on board was drowned: the captain, James Stewart, sixteen crew, eighty passengers and a huge number of pigs. Nobody knows why it came to grief just west of the River Dee. The North West Lightship had broken away from its moorings and possibly Captain

Stewart mistook the light on the Point of Ayr lighthouse for the North West Lightship.

It is said that the *Lord Blaney* ghost ship appears to foretell of a shipping disaster. It was seen before the *Connemara* and *Retriever* disaster (see Kilkeel in Chapter 3).

Michael G. Crawford in his book *Legendary Stories of the Carlingford Lough* described a sighting of the *Lord Blaney* as follows:

> We could see ... the tall masts and funnel of a steamer appear as if she were rising from the grey breast of the sea; then the mast head light shining like a star burst full upon us. The ship was tossed as if knocked about in a storm, although where she lay was dead calm. We could hear the sound of the swishing water against her side, and the wind blowing through her rigging, as she rolled onward on her course. When she came opposite the quays at Warrenpoint we saw a cloud of steam go up as if the whistle was shrieking a warning; then slowly she sank; her stern lights vanished beneath the waves.

SAMMY THE SMELLY POLTERGEIST

Sammy was associated with the Sinton family, a linen family who lived in a large Georgian house overlooking Tullylish, on the road between Banbridge and Gilford. When the old mill was no longer an economic proposition it lay empty for years and the daughters of the owner, Helen Sinton and her sister, used to dream of bringing it back to life.

Helen and her sister lived in the big house. There was a mysterious trunk in the attic. Nobody was sure who originally owned the trunk. They thought it had belonged to a long-dead great uncle who had gone to sea and had a wooden leg. All anyone knew about the trunk was that it moved around. It would be placed in one spot in the attic and some time later would be found somewhere else. People occupying the room beneath the attic heard it thumping about on the floor above them in the middle of the night.

Eventually, Helen married Raymond Boyd and began raising her family in her old home. It proved to be a liability because of its size and the cost of repairs, so they decided to move across the road and down the lane to live in part of the old mill. They renovated the old mill and breathed life into it by turning it into a restaurant, the Pot Belly, named after its old pot belly stove.

Helen is a very talented potter. She and her husband established Tullylish Pottery in the 1970s on the site of Banford bleach works on the banks of the River Bann. It's next to the Pot Belly restaurant, approximately 4 miles from Banbridge. Helen is inspired by Celtic culture. Her sculptures and tableware are individually handcrafted to an exceptionally high standard. No two pieces are identical, and the designs are continually evolving and changing. Helen's one-off hand-sculpted gallery pieces are much sought after by collectors, both in this country and abroad.

When the family moved house they took the old trunk and, unfortunately, the poltergeist came, too. They named him Sammy and he was a nuisance. He made his presence felt by causing a sickening smell to pervade the premises and time and time again he unlocked the front door! The family installed good locks and bolts. They made sure the door was firmly locked and bolted shut before they went to bed each night, but in the morning it was open. That was worrying because the pottery business is in an isolated position and was left wide open to intruders. That wasn't the only thing Sammy did. The Boyds had a safe and they didn't have the key for it. Sammy used to lock it! That was a terrible nuisance because they had to send for a locksmith to come and open it, a time-consuming and expensive exercise.

Eventually, the Boyds invited a priest to come and attempt to exorcise Sammy. The priest succeeded, Sammy hasn't bothered them since and Helen has been able to continue her pottery business in peace.

The old linen mill is situated in a spectacular environment steeped in character and history. If you want to get creative and mucky you can book an individual four-hour session with Helen and learn how to make pottery without being bothered by Sammy's ghost.

The oral tradition of the Sinton family was that Sammy had a wooden leg. Nobody took that seriously until another branch of the family found a wooden leg in their attic! Strange?

THE GHOST ON THE M1

Ireland's first motorway, opened on 10 July 1962, ran between Belfast and Lisburn, eventually being extended to reach Dungannon. It was possible to travel from Belfast to Lisburn and not see a single car. Times have changed! It's a very busy road now.

Local people didn't know about the rules and regulations for driving on a motorway! I remember seeing senior citizens, overcome with awe at such a wide road, driving slowly up the middle, blocking both lanes and admiring the scenery! Others stopped and picked mushrooms growing in the grass verges at the sides of the road and in the central reservation.

Although the new M1 between Belfast and Lisburn must have been the safest road in the British Isles, it didn't take it long to gain a resident ghost – a woman who's been spotted wandering along the side of the road on wet, stormy nights.

One dark, wet night shortly after the M1 opened, a man was driving slowly and carefully towards Belfast because visibility was bad. Suddenly and to his great surprise he saw a woman walking along the hard shoulder without either a raincoat or an umbrella. She looked lost. He stopped the car, wound down the window and asked, 'Would you like a lift?' She said she would, so he reached over and opened the door. She climbed in and he noticed she was wearing black high-heeled shoes and a very nice tweed suit with an unusual brooch. He reached over and closed the door.

They had a pleasant conversation about the weather before he commented on her brooch.

She said, 'I love that brooch. It was the first present my boyfriend gave me. Now we're engaged to be married.'

He congratulated her and hoped she'd have a long and happy married life. As they approached the outskirts of Belfast he asked her where she lived and she gave her address in one of the side streets off the Ormeau Road.

The car reached the roundabout at the end of the motorway. The rain was pelting down, making visibility even worse, so he spent several minutes concentrating on his driving. He turned towards the woman and found the seat was empty.

The man was very upset. He wondered if the woman had got out of the car without him noticing. Perhaps she'd doubted his intentions or something. He was worried so retraced his route to see if he could find her. She was nowhere to be seen.

During the next few days he worried about his passenger, remembered her address and decided to go and see if she was all right. The door of her home was opened by a pleasant elderly lady, who listened to what he had to say and invited him in. She sat him down before a roaring fire and gave him a cup of tea before saying, 'What I have to say will probably shock you. I want you to know that you're not the only person to give a lift to my daughter. She was killed in an accident on the M1 four weeks ago.'

GHOSTS ON THE ROAD BETWEEN NEWRY AND WARRENPOINT

There's an Elizabethan tower beside the lough on the right-hand side of the road when travelling from Newry to Warrenpoint. It is said to be haunted by the ghosts of Lazara and her lover, who may be seen in the waters of the lough on wild stormy nights.

The young couple were attempting to elope, drifting quietly past the tower in a rowing boat. Unfortunately, they were spotted by one of the guards. He fired an arrow that hit Lazara's lover, who fell into the water and drowned.

Lazara was overcome with grief. She didn't think of escaping but crouched in the bottom of the boat, weeping her heart out.

As a result, she was captured and held prisoner in the tower. She was the daughter of the chief of the Magennis Clan and a valuable hostage.

Lazara was very beautiful and one of the guards fell in love with her. She repelled his advances and he said, 'Marry me or I will have you tortured and flung in the dungeon. You can have a week to make up your mind. Marry me or certain death!'

When he came to get Lazara she eluded him by hiding behind the door and escaped by running up the stairs to the roof. He followed. She looked over the parapet and saw the waves crashing against the rocks below. Her dead lover appeared in the water, held out his arms and shouted, 'Jump! Jump Lazara! Come on darling, come to me.' Lazara jumped and the couple haunt the waters of Carlingford Lough around the Elizabethan tower.

That stretch of road is also reputedly haunted by the ghosts of fourteen British Army soldiers, who were murdered by the IRA on 27 August 1979. They were patrolling the road when rockets were fired at them from the other side of Carlingford Lough – that is, from the Irish Republic, which is under a different jurisdiction than Northern Ireland. The soldiers' ghosts stop cars and search them, but if you look back you'll find nobody's there!

HOUSE OF THE HELLFIRE CLUB

Local historian Frank O'Dowd told me about the actions of members of the Hellfire Club who once lived between Lurgan and Gilford. A member of the Hellfire Club owned a large, very beautiful house a mile or so past Ballydugan Pottery and Frank took me to see it.

The house was on the right-hand side of the road when travelling towards Lurgan on the road between Gilford and Lurgan. It's approached by a long tree-lined drive, leading to a cream-coloured house that surprised me by being in good order. It was a beautifully proportioned late Victorian or early Edwardian building, with bay windows and a lovely conservatory at one side.

I shivered when I saw it. There was an incredibly evil atmosphere. Frank smiled and said, 'I see that house gives you the creeps!' I agreed. He said it affected him the same way and that no occupant had been able to stay long in it since the last owner, a member of the Hellfire Club who died in the 1920s or early '30s. After that all subsequent occupants had bad luck. They died young, went bankrupt or left because they felt the house was cursed.

Frank said, 'The member of the Hellfire Club sold his soul to the Devil, lost his money and ended up with only a chauffeur to care for him. As he lay dying his chauffeur sat beside him and said afterwards, "When my master's soul left his body a large black dog jumped out of the bed and ran down the stairs."'

CURSES

Frank O'Dowd also told me about a farmer, who, although he was very near his home suddenly felt thirsty and asked a neighbour for a drink of water. The neighbour was very annoyed and put a curse on him. As a result, the poor man spent the whole night walking the 1 mile to his farm!

Another tale tells of a curse put on a farmer's hayrick, making it impossible to harvest anything grown on that spot.

10

BIG HOUSES, FAMOUS GARDENS AND THE MOURNES

BLOOMVALE HOUSE (BALLYDUGAN POTTERY)

Bloomvale House is an historic grade II listed thatched house built in 1785. Its first owner was a Huguenot called Gasgoine, who was a wealthy linen merchant. The house is interesting because few houses of similar type have survived. They fall between two stools, not being large and grand enough to be classed as stately homes and too big to be a rural cottage.

The original owner wasn't a mill owner. He was a 'middleman'. He bought linen from the many out-weavers living in local cottages, did the final processing of the cloth and sold it. The house became a centre for excellent craft work.

The present owner, Sean O'Dowd, bought and restored the premises in 1996 and renamed it Ballydugan Pottery, so the tradition of producing craft work continues to the present day. Each piece of pottery, like the original linen, is designed to be beautiful, strong and useful. As well as the pottery, the building contains a craft shop, a coffee lounge and a restaurant. It's on the road between Gilford and Lurgan and is well worth a visit.

SEAFORDE GARDENS AND
TROPICAL BUTTERFLY HOUSE

Forgive me for writing about this garden from a very personal point of view. I feel emotionally involved with the garden and think that's a common reaction.

The first time I visited Seaforde Gardens I was depressed. I parked my car and nearly jumped out of my skin, because I thought I heard a banshee! Then I couldn't help laughing. I realised the screeching wasn't a banshee – it was caused by peacocks!

I wandered around the butterfly house and at one point had three butterflies resting on me. They were incredibly beautiful. I began to relax and watched what seemed like hundreds of butterflies flitting around. Eventually I decided I'd spent enough time inside and would like a wee dander around the gardens. That 'wee dander' turned into a visit of several hours, during which I was enchanted.

The gardens have a much-loved, personal feel. I felt friendly spirits from the past were accompanying me as I admired specimens of ceanothus, with its evergreen foliage and blue flowers and the tall blue spikes of camassia. I was no longer depressed. I went to the nursery and had a chat with a gentleman I now realise was Patrick Forde himself. I thought he was just a very knowledgeable employee.

Seaforde Gardens has been in the Forde family since 1637, when King Charles I granted land to Sir Patrick's ancestor, Mathew Forde. The pretty village of Seaforde has grown up near the gardens. It has an old courthouse and almshouses clustered around the parish church, which was built by Colonel Mathew Forde MP in 1720. The almshouses originally housed six elderly people and they still look in excellent condition.

The late owner, Patrick Forde, inherited the demesne from his father in 1961. His wife, Lady Anthea Forde, said:

> The garden was a complete shambles. The walled garden
> was a terrible mess with derelict glasshouses, it was covered

in brambles and I kept a donkey there! Patrick was a very keen plantsman in those days. He had an amazing vision of what he wanted the restored gardens to look like. I love insects and the tropical butterfly house was my idea.

Today the walled garden is a delightful mix of Classical and Romantic styles with magnolias, lilies, cherries and a hornbeam maze with seats to rest the weary in the middle. Patrick and Lady Anthea designed it to celebrate their first ten years of marriage and a friend asked, 'Is that a symbol of marriage? Something that's very easy to get into and difficult to get out of!'

The glasshouses have been cleared and recycled, and the copper heating pipes were used to build a summer house, with a copper tree fashioned against the back wall. The tree originally had leaves but unfortunately members of the public have removed most of them, but in spite of the vandalism it still looks stunning. Swallows nest in the roof, so whenever they're in residence the garden seat is temporarily removed.

In 1992 a mogul tower was built near the summer house. A climb up the stairs is rewarded by a beautiful view over the garden.

The walled garden contains a national collection of eucryphias. There are twenty-one varieties planted in two walks. They are mostly evergreen trees that, in autumn, look magnificent as they become covered in white flowers with yellow stamens.

A door leads out of the walled garden into the pheasantry. Its mind-blowing! There's a tree brought back from the Crimean War by an ancestor of Patrick Forde who served in the Light Brigade. Luckily, he missed the charge because he was organising races at Sebastopol!

Seaforde Gardens has other rare plants because Patrick Forde travelled to Tibet, India, China and Vietnam and brought back seeds. They germinated and are thriving. He was a generous man who was delighted when asked to share his expertise.

Lady Anthea Forde is ably carrying on the family tradition, travelling widely, studying gardens in faraway places and bringing expertise back home. As a result, Ireland, especially Seaforde, is a richer place.

CASTLE WARD

Castle Ward is an eccentric home built in 1760 by an unknown architect for its owner, Bernard Ward, later 1st Viscount Bangor, and is today run by the National Trust.

Lord Bangor and his wife, Lady Anne, could not agree about anything, never mind the style of their house! As a result, the entrance façade to the east is built in Palladian style, as are the rooms behind it, while the part of the house facing to the west is Gothic.

The property contains many interesting records from the past, including a book collection reflecting the interests of the family. The Castle Ward papers record, among other fascinating details, that Lady Sophia spent £21 on a lace head (these are the high cushions used in Queen Anne's time, and later, to put under their hair to make their heads look huge, as shown in portraits of the period). £21 would have been sufficient to feed a farming family comfortably for a year!

There's a story in the Bangor family about one of the Lady Clanwilliams, who wore her lace head for months. When it was eventually removed there was a family of mice living inside it!

Castle Ward has an interesting collection of family portraits by Strickland Lowry, Lely, Batoni, Romney and Ramsay, as well as paintings by Irish landscape artists Ashford and Fisher depicting the house as it was in the eighteenth century. There's also an occasional special exhibit of Mary Ward's work as a naturalist, microscopist and amateur illustrator. Victorians were very keen on taxidermy and a display reflecting this interest includes five cases of stuffed squirrels called 'The Pugilists' in a boxing ring sequence. There's also a Russian bear, shot in 1880 by Mr Kennedy and said to have been swapped for the 5th Lord Bangor's daughter!

Some of the books in the collection were inherited from the Hamiltons of Bangor and Killyleagh Castle. They go back to the time of the Plantation of the Ards Peninsula in 1607.

The house contains 2,418 books, with about 800 predating 1801, and a magnificent coloured set of the first edition *Ordnance Survey of County Down*.

Castle Ward provides a good family day out in a beautiful setting on the shore of Strangford Lough. There you can walk or cycle along 34km of trails that stretch from Temple Water along the ornamental canal to Audley's Castle, a tower house built in the fifteenth century.

The woodlands are sheltered and contain many rare plants and a rich variety of wildlife.

Clearsky Adventure is an interesting concept. It's possible, with their help, to build a raft and venture out on the lough, or hire a canoe or bike.

There's a second-hand bookshop and the possibility of visiting resident artists' studios and watch them at work.

The barn has children's crafts, lots of ride-on tractors and a playroom. The weans (children) may enjoy a visit to the farmyard with its chickens, ducks and pygmy goats. You could take them to check out the Secret Nature Shore Trail, with its mile-long stretch of nature and activities.

The farmyard was one of the locations for Winterfell in *Game of Thrones*.

ROWALLANE

Rowallane, Saintfield, is a beautiful garden owned by the National Trust and surrounding a house built by the Revd John Moore during the nineteenth century.

The Revd Moore was a keen gardener, who laid the foundation of the garden. He left the property to his nephew, Hugh Armytage Moore, who developed his uncle's creation. It's a mixture of formal and informal places containing many rare plants and renowned for the beauty of its rhododendron and azalea displays in spring and early summer.

MOUNT STEWART

Mount Stewart, on the shores of Strangford Lough and owned today by the National Trust, once belonged to the Londonderry family, who played a major part in local and international history, and is still a much-loved family home.

The mild climate of Strangford Lough enables rare and tender plants to thrive. Edith, Lady Londonderry had a passion for bold planting schemes and the garden she created has consistently been voted one of the top ten in the world. The property is extensive, with an attractive shop and pleasant tea rooms.

The formal gardens are divided into four separate parts, the Shamrock Garden, the Italian Garden, the Mairi Garden and the Spanish Garden.

The Shamrock Garden reflects Lady Edith's love of Irish mythology and its surrounding topiary hedge is a beautifully depicted children's story. There's a topiary statue depicting a Formorian (a half-human, half-demon) associated with Strangford Lough. (Folklore credits St Patrick with banishing a Formorian in the River Lagan, see Chapter 4.) The rose garden is being restored and the fernery has been extended.

The wider demesne has miles of walking trails and a landscape that appears lost in time. A visit to the Temple of the Winds is a must. It's a very romantic place to hold a wedding.

The nineteenth-century house has recently undergone an £8 million restoration programme. There are collections of national and international significance as well as one of the most significant silver displays in the Trust's care. Works by Brock, Lawrence and Stubbs are on display. The Central Hall floor has been restored, as has the stunning Rome bedroom. Visitors can either take a guided tour or explore the house at their leisure (there are attendants in every room who are more than willing to answer questions). It is well worth a day's visit.

THE KINGDOM OF MOURNE

The Kingdom of Mourne got its name when it was seized by a tribe of MacMahons, who came from Monaghan during the twelfth century. They were descended from Colla Nais, King of Ireland 323–326 AD. Eventually they were defeated by the Anglo-Normans, who built two strongholds: Dundrum Castle and Greencastle. The Kingdom was given to the abbey at Newry in the twelfth century. In the sixteenth century, Queen Elizabeth I appointed Nicholas Bagenal as Marshall of the Army in Ireland (1547). He was given a lease of the Abbot's House in Newry, which was originally part of the Cisterian Abbey. He demolished the Abbot's House and replaced it by building his own Bagenal's Castle. It was originally a fortified house and is now a museum (see Newry in Chapter 3).

The old saying 'twelve miles of Mourne' arose because the Anglo-Norman Lordship or Barony of Mourne had the same boundaries as the Celtic kingdom. The boundaries are marked by two rivers, the Cassy Water (now marked on maps as the Causeway Water) and St Patrick's Stream, so-called because legend has it that St Patrick never went across it. Tradition states he never visited the Kingdom of Mourne because it was a close community with a strong belief in pagan gods. Any normal saint (see Chapter 4) would have cursed it, but he blessed it. When he reached the road leading around the shore at the bottom of the mountains he threw his brogue along it and said, 'May peace reign evermore in their region.' (Folklore claims it landed at Kilhornan, near Annalong.) There's another version of this story that says St Patrick blessed the area at Clonlaoc, approximately a mile from Warrenpoint on the Dromore Road. There's a high cross in the prehistoric cemetery, along with two modern crosses. Local tradition has it the ancient high cross was put on the spot where St Patrick stood and the authorities wanted to erect it in Newry marketplace. They made many attempts but horses pulling the cart carrying the cross always became weak at Puss's Hill and had to rest overnight. Next morning the cross would have disappeared and gone back to Clonlaoc cemetery!

The Kingdom of Mourne is a peaceful place, welcoming strangers and accepting their individual differences in appearance and beliefs.

The Mountains of Mourne inspired Percy French to write his famous song, also called 'The Mountains of Mourne'.

Slieve Donard towers above Newcastle and at 2,789ft is the highest mountain in Northern Ireland. It gets its name after a chieftain called Donard, who lived at Rath Murbolg (the present Maghera). Folklore says St Patrick succeeded in converting St Donard to Christianity by breathing life into a bull after it had been jointed and salted down!

St Donard is said to have founded two churches, one at Maghera and the other on top of Slieve Donard, which used to be visited by great numbers of pilgrims.

Donard's Cave, which is north of St Patrick's Stream, is reputed to run through the heart of the mountain up to a large chamber at the summit. Folklore says it's inadvisable to approach the summit that way because it makes St Donard angry. He appears fully dressed in his robes, scolds and says that's where he wants to live in peace without any disturbance until Judgement Day!

When travelling along the coastal road at the foot of Slieve Donard it's possible to see large boulders placed in a regular pattern along the shore. They were used to encourage the growth of seaweed (wrack). Seaweed is an excellent fertiliser. In the past the wrack roads (straight lanes leading from the main road to the shore) were used by farmers to bring carts down to the shore to collect the wrack and spread it on their land to improve its fertility. Each farmer had his own patch of wrack and

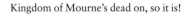

Kingdom of Mourne's dead on, so it is!

sometimes one farmer would steal another one's wrack, resulting in a fight on the shore!

Over time the name 'Kingdom of MacMahon' was shortened to Kingdom of Mourne. The area has a reputation for friendly generous hospitality. Frank Marshall recorded an old saying about the region, 'Kindly Mourne, where if you ask for a drink of water they'll fry you bacon.'

The Kingdom of Mourne has been designated as an area of outstanding natural beauty and contains many forest parks, including the following.

TULLYMORE FOREST PARK

Until the mid-seventeenth century the Magennis family owned Upper Iveagh, then Ellen Magennis, who owned the land around Tullymore, married William Hamilton, whose family had originally come from Lanarkshire. (Most Scottish planters married into local Irish families.) Their son, James Hamilton, married Anne Mordant, whose son James was given the title of 1st Earl of Clanbrassill. He was a keen florist and horticulturalist who began an arboretum of rare and beautiful trees. The landscape is very diverse and the park is proactively managed to ensure the survival of rare species, including the red squirrel.

The property was used by the army during the Second World War. The owners, in common with the majority of owners of stately homes at the time, found upkeep prohibitive so they sold it to the Forestry Division and went to live in England. The house fell into disrepair and was demolished in 1952.

Tullymore was the first state forest to be designated a forest park. It was opened to the public in 1955. It contains marked trails of various lengths, including one that tradition states was once walked by St Patrick himself.

James, the 2nd Earl of Clanbrassill, extended the house and build Gothic Gate in 1786. The hermitage was built beside the River Shimna as a memorial to his friend, the Marquis of Monthermer.

It is thought that two Clanbrassill earls, who were keen amateur architects, were helped by an architect from Durham to design the mansion, gates, follies and bridges. They are very unusual and otherworldly.

Tullymore Forest Park provided locations for HBO's award-winning television series *Game of Thrones*. They feature in Westeros as the haunted forest north of the wall, the Wolfswood near Winterfell, the Kingsroad near Castle Black, and a forest near the Dreadfort.

It's possible to book a guided location trek for *Game of Thrones*. The tour isn't included in the park's entrance fee. A calendar of dates and prices is available on their website. It starts from the car park at 3 p.m. and is an 'immersive' experience as Stark cloaks are provided at no extra cost.

CASTLEWELLAN FOREST PARK

Castlewellan Forest Park has a stunning setting against the background of the Mourne Mountains. It contains Northern Ireland's National Arboretum, beautiful gardens, a lake, scenic walking trails, mountain bike trails, an equestrian centre, activities for children, a site for caravans and camping, and a peace maze.

Different people feel different things about mazes. All I can say is: never again! My family and I went into the so-called 'peace maze' and spent most of the afternoon arguing about how to get out! We'd have been trapped in there yet if a kindly man hasn't helped us escape.

The arboretum contains a collection of outstanding trees and shrubs established by a previous owner of the property, Hugh Annesley. It attracts tree enthusiasts from around the world.

Hugh was a keen photographer and his work has been preserved, so it's possible to trace the history of the gardens from the early days of photography in the nineteenth century to the present day.

The gardens were established by the Magennis family along with a brewery about 1730.

William Annesley bought the property in 1741 and built a wall across the centre. The upper half of the wall supported fruit trees while the lower part was decorative. He also established a formal pleasure garden.

The castle was built by William Richard Annesley in the 1850s. He added two fountains, flights of steps and a viewing point where the present glass houses are situated.

DRUMKEERAGH FOREST PARK

Drumkeeragh Forest Park, around the foot of Slieve Croob and the source of the River Lagan, is said to be haunted by the ghost of Penny McAllister.

Penny was the wife of an army officer who was having an affair with a Greenfinch called Susan Christie. When he tried to end the affair, Susan became jealous. She befriended Penny, invited her for a walk in Drumkeeragh Forest on 27 March 1991 and cut her throat. Susan gave herself a minor leg injury, tore her own clothes and reported Penny's death to the police. She said they'd been attacked by a mad, knife-wielding man and had only escaped by kneeing him in the groin. The police uncovered evidence pointing to the truth. Susan was tried and sentenced to nine years in prison. She was released in December 1995, having served five years, after being granted remission for good behaviour.

THE SILENT VALLEY

The City of Belfast grew during the eighteenth century and needed more water, so it was decided to build a reservoir. An engineer called Luke Livingstone McCassey choose a valley in the heart of the Mourne Mountains as a suitable source because of the purity of its waters. Personally speaking, I never realised how good water from the Silent Valley was until I moved to a house outside the catchment area. I never settled in my 'new' house because the water smelt like diluted toilet cleaner! It was horrible!

The Silent Valley is said to have been named because the disruption and noise during construction caused the birds to stop singing. The birds have come back but the valley retains a sense of peace and solitude, which is surprising because it attracts 50,000 visitors a year! The mountains provide a stunning backdrop and the reservoir is surrounded by a beautifully landscaped garden. There are information and educational conference centres which are housed in two old-style colonial bungalows with beautiful views.

During the first stage of construction water was taken from the Annalong and Kilkeel Rivers and piped to a reservoir at Carryduff at a rate of 10 million gallons per day. A reservoir was built across the Kilkeel River during the second stage of construction, which supplied another 10 million gallons of water a day. The third stage of construction provided a storage reservoir that retained water from the Annalong River. As a result, the Silent Valley was able to supply Belfast with a total of 30,000 gallons of water per day in the 1930s.

The site contains a variety of walking loops of varying difficulty.

The Mourne Wall was built to enclose the Silent Valley's catchment area between 1904 and 1922. It's 22 miles long, stands 1.5m high and is approximately 1m wide. It passes over fifteen of the Mourne's summits. It's constructed of Mourne granite using traditional drystone walling techniques. The whole scheme, including the wall, cost in excess of £2 million. It was a huge engineering project. Materials were supplied by building a railway that ran the 4.5 miles from Annalong Harbour to the Silent Valley. It transported hundreds of men, over a million tons of material, as well as heavy machinery.

The Silent Valley was a godsend for the 2,000 men from Mourne that it employed as it provided work during the Great Depression. The only other jobs available at the time were on fishing boats or in quarries. Unfortunately, eight men lost their lives during construction.

NEWRY CANAL

Newry Canal was the first summit-level canal to be built in the British Isles. It predated the famous Bridgewater Canal and linked Carlingford Lough and the Irish Sea with the coalfields in Tyrone, via the River Bann and Lough Neagh. A ship canal was opened near Newry in 1769. At first the canal and Newry, flourished, having been enlarged to allow 5,000-ton ships to reach Newry. Gradually it stopped being used and was closed in 1966. It has recently been reopened for pleasure craft and has become a haven for wildlife. It forms part of the National Cycle Network and the towpath also acts as a long-distance footpath. Many difficulties were encountered during the restoration process, such as a farmer between Scarva and Portadown who didn't like the idea of people walking near his land. He put a fence across the towpath and housed a ferocious bull on the other side!

BIBLIOGRAPHY

Bassett, George Henry, *County Down One Hundred Years Ago: A Guide and Directory, 1886*, Friar's Bush Press, 1988.

Bates, Nora, *Up the Down Street*, Adare Press, 1994.

Breen, Dermot, *The Edge: Walking the Ulster Way with my Angels and Demons*, Shanway Press, 1917.

Crawford, Michael G., *Legendary Stories of the Carlingford Lough District*, V.G. Havern, Warrenpoint, 1965.

Doonan, Tommy, '*Caught by a U-Boat at Sea: A Kilkeel Fishing Boat was Sunk Without Loss of a Single Life*', *Ulster Annual*, 1974.

Evans, E. Estyn, *Mourne Country*, Dundalgan Press, Dundalk, 1989.

Heyward, Richard, *In Praise of Ulster*, Wm Mullan & Son, 1938.

Laudon, Jack, *Oh Rare Amanda*, London, Chatto and Windus, 1954.

Lyttle W.G., *The Smugglers of Strangford Lough*, first published in the *North Down Herald* and later published in book form around 1890. Re-published Mourne Observer Press, with Appendix, 1979.

Marshall, John J., *Popular Rhymes and Sayings of Ireland*, first published in 1904.

McBride, Doreen, *What They Did With Plants*, Adare Press, 1991.

Mourne Maritime Visitor Centre, Kilkeel Harbour and Greenore Maritime Museum, The SS *Connemara* and *Retriever* Disaster funded by the International Fund for Ireland.

McCorry, Francis Xavier, *A Portrait of West County Down*, self-published, 2013.

McDonnell, Hector, *St Patrick: His Life and Legend*, Wooden Books Ltd, 2007.

McIlroy, Eric, *Dolly Munroe: The Famous Irish Beauty*, Poyntz and District Local History Society Magazine, No.9, 2003.

Scott, Archdeacon John, 'Inspired: Holy Trinity Parish Church', *Banbridge Chronicle*, June 2011.

Seaby, W.A, *Great Irishmen: An Exhibition of Portraits of Great Irishmen and Women*, Ulster Museum Belfast Publication, No. 173, 1965.

Stevenson, John, *Two Centuries of Life in County Down 1600–1800*, The White Row Press, 1990.

Thackeray, William Makepeace, *The Irish Sketchbook of 1842* (first published 1843), Nonsuch Publishing Ltd, 2005.

Turner, Brian, *Patrick Patron Saint of Ireland*, County Down Museum Information Sheet no 3, Down County Museum, Downpatrick, 2009.

Warner, Alan, *Walking the Ulster Way*, Appletree Press,1989.